MW00963692

A Study Guide to
Service Catalogue

From the Principles of ITIL® V3

London: TSO

Published by TSO (The Stationery Office)
and available from:
Online
www.tsoshop.co.uk

Mail, Telephone, Fax & E-mail
TSO
PO Box 29, Norwich, NR3 1GN
Telephone orders/General enquiries:
0870 600 5522
Fax orders: 0870 600 5533
E-mail: customer.services@tso.co.uk
Textphone 0870 240 3701

TSO@Blackwell and other Accredited Agents

Customers can also order publications from:
TSO Ireland
16 Arthur Street, Belfast BT1 4GD
Tel 028 9023 8451 Fax 028 9023 5401

Service Catalogue Study Guide

© APMG-International 2010
All rights reserved, no part of this publication
may be reproduced in any form or by any
means without the express permission of APMG-
International.

Information contained in this publication is
believed to be correct at time of production.
Whilst care has been taken to ensure that the
information is accurate, the publisher can accept
no responsibility for any errors or omissions.
APMG-International
Sword House
Totteridge Road
High Wycombe
HP13 6DG
Contact; servicedesk@apmgroup.co.uk
Web; www.apmg-international.com

First edition 2010
ISBN 9780117063648

ITIL® is a Registered Trade Mark of the Office of
Government Commerce in the United Kingdom
and other countries
All reproduced ITIL material within this
publication is licensed © Crown copyright
material is reproduced with the permission of
the Controller of HMSO and Queen's Printer for
Scotland

Acknowledgements
AUTHOR
Hank Marquis, Global Knowledge

REVIEWERS
Pierre Bernard, Pink Elephant
Leah Radstone, APMG

EDITOR
Elaine Taylor

Contents

List of figures

List of tables

Section 1 – INTRODUCTION TO SERVICE CATALOGUE CONCEPTS

SCM:01

We have arrived at a point in history where IT services are prevalent throughout virtually all businesses. Most enterprises and many government functions are totally dependent upon reliable and responsive IT services to underpin vital business, community and social functions. IT services have become mainstream and managing them to deliver value is the core message of ITIL v3.

Managing IT by service instead of by technology was the message of ITIL v2. ITIL v3 continues to support the increasing importance of IT service management by extending IT management to focus on facilitating business value. To that end, ITIL v3 has promoted the Service Catalogue from an important output of the Service Level Management process in ITIL v2 to its own process, the Service Catalogue Management process. This elevation and emphasis is a direct result of the growing requirement for business and IT to work together sharing data, information and knowledge about demand for services, service capabilities and patterns of business activity and demand.

Service Catalogue Management is now a very important management field complete with its own unique terminology and vital concepts. Many terms are familiar from previous versions of ITIL, some from related business disciplines, and others are new. Learning about this new guidance regarding roles, responsibilities, activities, and metrics is critical to successfully deploying a Service Catalogue Management process. However, the terms Service Asset, Utility, Warranty, Capabilities, Resources and other new definitions are more than words; they have a profound impact when it comes to aligning IT and business, delivering business outcomes, and managing a portfolio of IT and business services.

The purpose of a Service Catalogue is first and foremost a means of giving business the visibility and control that it needs to justify, make and validate sound investments. The Service Catalogue also establishes the value of IT services to the business as it provides IT value in the form of

helping to deliver value on investment, as well as managing limited resources in the most effective and efficient ways.

This section introduces the new terms and concepts in the ITIL v3 Service Catalogue Management process in the context of organizational value, value to the business as well as value to IT, as the chapter sets the stage for managing a vibrant Service Catalogue.

1.1 WHAT ARE SERVICES?
1.1.1 The value proposition

Service
A service is a means of delivering value to customers by facilitating the outcomes customers want to achieve without the ownership of specific costs and risks.

Services are a means of delivering value to customers by facilitating outcomes customers want to achieve without the ownership of specific costs and **risks**. **Outcomes** are possible from the **performance** of tasks and are limited by the presence of certain constraints. Broadly speaking, services facilitate outcomes by enhancing the performance and by reducing the grip of constraints. The result is an increase in the possibility of desired outcomes. While some services enhance performance of tasks, others have a more direct **impact**. They perform the task itself.

The preceding paragraph is not just a definition, as it is a recurring pattern found in a wide range of services. Patterns are useful for managing complexity, costs, flexibility and variety. They are generic structures useful to make an idea work in a wide range of **environments** and situations. In each instance the pattern is applied with variations that make the idea effective, economical, or simply useful in that particular case.

Take, for example, the generalized pattern of a storage **system**. Storage is useful for holding, organizing or securing **assets** within the context of some **activity**, task or performance. Storage also creates useful conditions such as ease of access, efficient **organization** or security from **threats**. This simple pattern is inherent in many types of storage services, each specialized to support a particular type of **outcome** for customers.

For various reasons, customers seek outcomes but do not wish to have accountability or ownership of all the associated costs and risks. For example, a **business unit** needs a terabyte of secure storage to support its online shopping system. From a strategic perspective, it wants the staff, equipment, facilities and infrastructure for a terabyte of storage to remain within its span of **control**. It does not want, however, to be accountable for all the associated costs and risks, real or nominal, actual or perceived. Fortunately, there is a group within the **business** with specialized knowledge and experience in large-scale storage systems, and the confidence to control the associated costs and risks. The business unit agrees to pay for the storage **service** provided by the group under specific terms and conditions.

The business unit remains responsible for the **fulfilment** of online purchase orders. It is not responsible for the **operation** and maintenance of fault-tolerant configurations of storage devices, dedicated and redundant power supplies, qualified personnel, or the security of the building perimeter, administrative expenses, insurance, **compliance** with safety regulations, contingency measures, or the optimization problem of idle **capacity** for unexpected surges in demand. The **design** complexity, **operational** uncertainties, and technical trade-offs associated with maintaining

reliable high-**performance** storage **systems** lead to costs and risks the business unit is simply not willing to own. The **service provider** assumes ownership and allocates those costs and risks to every unit of storage utilized by the business and any other customers of the storage **service**.

1.1.2 Value composition

From the customer's perspective, value consists of two primary elements: *utility* or fitness for purpose and *warranty* or fitness for use. Utility is perceived by the customer from the attributes of the service that have a positive effect on the performance of tasks associated with desired outcomes. Removal or relaxation of constraints on performance is also perceived as a positive effect.

Warranty is derived from the positive effect being available when needed, in sufficient capacity or magnitude, and dependably in terms of continuity and security.

Utility is what the customer gets, and warranty is *how* it is delivered.

Customers cannot benefit from something that is **fit for purpose** but not fit for use, and vice versa. It is useful to separate the logic of utility from the logic of warranty for the purpose of design, development and improvement (Figure 1.1). Considering all the separate controllable inputs allows for a wider range of solutions to the problem of creating, maintaining and increasing value.

Take the case of the **business unit** utilizing the high-performance online storage service. For them the value is not just from the functionality

Figure 1.1 – Logic of value creation through services[1]

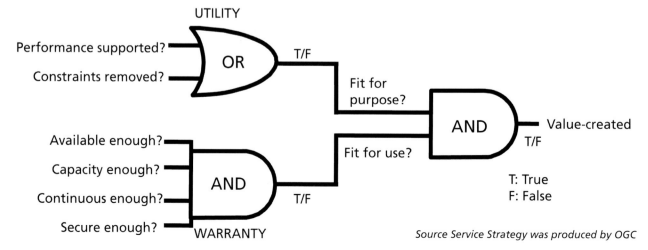

Source Service Strategy was produced by OGC

of online storage but also from easy access to no less than one terabyte of fault-tolerant storage, as and when needed, with **confidentiality**, **integrity**, and availability of data. Chapter 3 of Service Strategy provides further detail on the concepts of utility and warranty.

An **outcome**-based definition of service moves IT organizations beyond business-IT alignment towards business-IT integration. Internal dialogue and discussion on the meaning of services is an elementary step towards alignment and integration with a **customer's business**. Customer outcomes become the ultimate concern of product managers instead of the gathering of **requirements**, which is necessary but not sufficient. **Requirements** are generated for internal coordination and **control** only after customer outcomes are well understood. Chapter 4 of *Service Strategy* provides detail on the practical use of outcome-based definitions.

1.1.3 The business process

Business outcomes are produced by **business processes** governed by **objectives**, policies and constraints. The processes are supported by **resources** including people, knowledge, **applications** and infrastructure. Workflow coordinates the execution of tasks and flow of control between resources, and intervening action to ensure adequate **performance** and desired outcomes. **Business processes** are particularly important from a **service management** perspective. They apply the **organization's** cumulative knowledge and experience to the achievement of a particular outcome.

1.2   THE SERVICE LIFECYCLE

Case study 1: *Telecommunication services*
Some time during the 1990s, a large internet **service provider** switched its internet service offerings from variable **pricing** to all-you-can-use fixed pricing. The strategic intent was to differentiate from competitor services through superior pricing **plans**. The **service strategy** worked exceedingly well – customers flocked to sign up. The outcomes, however, included large numbers of customers facing congestion or the inability to log on.

Why was there such a disconnection between the **strategy** and operations?

(Answer at the end of the chapter)

The lifecycle
The architecture of the **ITIL** core is based on a service **lifecycle**. Each volume of the core is represented in the service lifecycle (Figure 1.2). **Service design**, **service transition** and **service operation** are progressive phases of the lifecycle that represent **change** and transformation. Service strategy represents policies and **objectives**. **Continual service improvement** represents learning and improvement.

Figure 1.2 – The service lifecycle [2]

Source Service Strategy was produced by OGC

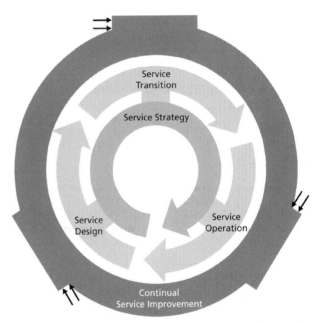

Service strategy (SS) is the axis around which the lifecycle rotates. Service design (SD), **service transition** (ST), and **service operation** (SO) implement strategy. **Continual service improvement** (CSI) helps place and prioritize improvement **programmes** and projects based on strategic objectives.

1.2.1 Lifecycle and systems thinking
While feedback samples output to influence future action, structure is essential for organizing unrelated information. Without structure, our **service management** knowledge is merely a collection of observations, practices and conflicting goals. The structure of the service lifecycle is an organizing framework. Processes

describe how things change, whereas structure describes how they are connected. Structure determines behaviour. Altering the structure of service management can be more effective than simply controlling discrete events. Without structure, it is difficult to learn from experience. It is difficult to use the past to educate for the future. We believe we can learn from experience but we never directly confront many of the most important consequences of our actions.

1.2.2 Great leverage for sustainable change lies in structure

The service lifecycle is a comprehensive approach to service management: seeking to understand its structure, the interconnections between all its components, and how changes in any area will affect the whole system and its constituent parts over time. It is an organizing framework designed for sustainable performance.

1.2.3 Today's problem is often created by yesterday's solution

A systems approach to service management ensures learning and improvement through a big-picture view of services and service management. It extends the management horizon and provides a sustainable long-term approach.

1.3 SERVICE MANAGEMENT

Information technology (IT) is a commonly used term that changes meaning with context. From the first perspective, IT systems, applications, and infrastructure are components or sub-assemblies of a larger product. They enable or are embedded in processes and services. From the second perspective, IT is an organization with its own set of capabilities and resources. IT organizations can be of various types, such as business functions, shared services units, and enterprise-level core units.

From the third perspective, IT is a category of services utilized by business. They are typically IT applications and infrastructure that are packaged and offered as services by internal IT organizations or external service providers. IT costs are treated as business expenses. From the fourth perspective, IT is a category of business assets that provide a stream of benefits for their owners, including but not limited to revenue, income and profit. IT costs are treated as investments.

Service Design Package – see Service Design book glossary for details.

1.3.1 Service portfolio, pipeline and catalogue

The service portfolio represents the commitments and investments made by a service provider across all customers and market spaces. It represents present contractual commitments, new service development, and ongoing service improvement plans initiated by continual service improvement. The portfolio also includes third-party services, which are an integral part of service offerings to customers. Some third-party services are visible to the customers while others are not.

1.3.2 Service portfolio

The portfolio management approach helps managers prioritize investments and improve the allocation of resources. Changes to portfolios are governed by policies and procedures. Portfolios instil a certain financial discipline necessary to avoid making investments that will not yield value. Service portfolios represent the ability and readiness of a service provider to serve customers and market spaces. The service portfolio is divided into three phases: service catalogue, service pipeline and retired services (Figure 1.3).

The service portfolio represents all the resources presently engaged or being released in various phases of the service lifecycle. Each phase requires resources for completion of projects, initiatives and contracts. This is a very important governance aspect of service portfolio management (SPM). Entry, progress and exit are approved only with approved funding and a financial plan for recovering costs or showing profit as necessary. The portfolio should have the right mix of services in the pipeline and catalogue to secure the financial viability of the service provider. The service catalogue is the only part of the portfolio that recovers costs or earns profits.

In summary, SPM is about maximizing value while managing risks and costs. The value realization is derived from better service delivery and customer experiences. Through SPM, managers are better able to understand quality requirements and related delivery costs. They can then seek to reduce costs through alternative means while maintaining service quality. The SPM journey begins with documenting the organization's

Figure 1.3 – Service pipeline and service catalogue [3]

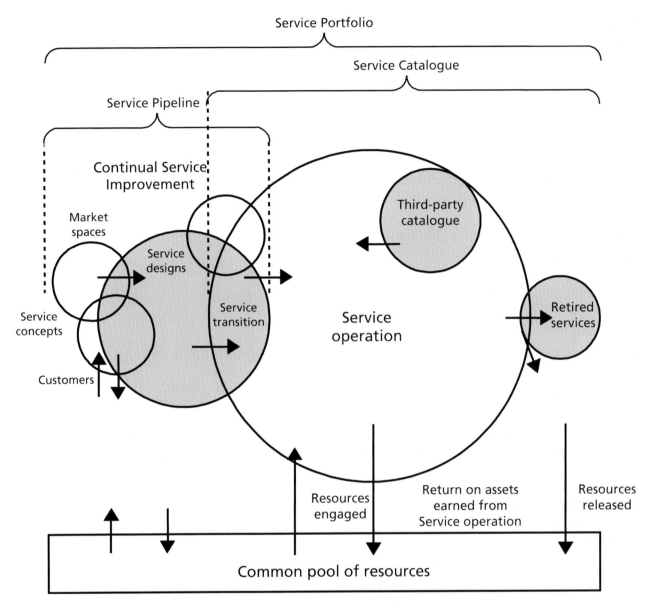

Area of circle is proportional to resources currently engaged in the lifecycle
phase (Service Portfolio and Financial Management)

Source Service Strategy was produced by OGC

standardized services, and as such has strong links
to **service level management**, particularly the
service catalogue.

1.3.3 Elements of a service portfolio and service catalogue

The **service catalogue** is the subset of the **service portfolio** visible to customers. It consists of
services presently active in the **service operation**
phase and those approved to be readily offered
to current or prospective customers. Items
can enter the service catalogue only after due
diligence has been performed on related costs
and risks. **Resources** are engaged to fully support

active services.

The catalogue is useful in developing suitable
solutions for customers from one or more services.
Items in the catalogue can be configured and
suitably priced to fulfil a particular need. The
service catalogue is an important tool for **service
strategy** because it is the virtual projection of the
service provider's actual and present capabilities.
Many customers are only interested in what the
provider can commit now, rather than in future.
The value of future possibilities is discounted in
the present.

It serves as a **service** order and demand channelling mechanism. It communicates and defines the policies, **guidelines** and accountability required for SPM. It defines the criteria for what services fall under SPM and the **objective** of each service. It acts as the acquisition portal for customers, including **pricing** and service-level commitments, and the terms and conditions for service provisioning. It is in the **service catalogue** that services are decomposed into **components**; it is where **assets**, processes and **systems** are introduced with entry points and terms for their use and provisioning. As providers may have many customers or serve many businesses, there may be multiple service catalogues projected from the service portfolio. In other words, a service catalogue is an expression of the provider's **operational capability** within the context of a customer or **market space**.

The service catalogue is also a visualization tool for SPM decisions. It is in the catalogue that demand for services comes together with the **capacity** to fulfil it. Customer assets attached to a **business outcome** are sources of demand. In particular, they have expectations of **utility** and warranty. If any items in the catalogue can fulfil those expectations, a connection is made resulting in a **service contract** or **agreement**. Catalogue items are clustered into lines of service (LOS) based on common patterns of business activity (PBA) they can support.

1.3.4 Service catalogue and demand management

LOS performing well are allocated additional **resources** to ensure continued **performance** and anticipate increases in demand for those services. Items performing above a financial threshold are deemed viable services. An effort is to be made to make them popular by introducing new attributes, new **service level packages** (SLP), improved matching with sources of demand, or by new **pricing** policies. If **performance** drops below a threshold, then they are marked for retirement. A new **service transition project** is initiated and a transition **plan** is drafted to phase out the service.

Services with poor financial performance may be retained in the catalogue with adequate justification. Some catalogue services may have **strategic** use of such contingency for another service and contractual obligations to a few early customers. Whatever the justification, it must be approved by senior leadership who may choose to subsidize. This issue differs with Type I (internal) providers who are often required to maintain a catalogue of service, regardless of their independent financial viability.

A subset of the **service catalogue** may be third-party or outsourced services. These are services that are offered to customers with varying levels of value addition or combination with other catalogue items. The third-party catalogue may consist of **core service packages** (CSP) and SLP. It extends the range of the service catalogue in terms of customers and **market spaces**. Third-party services may be used to address underserved or unserved demand until items in the **service pipeline** are phased into **operation**. They can also be used as a substitute for services being phased out of the catalogue. Sourcing is not only an important strategic option but can also be an **operational** necessity.

Candidate **suppliers** of the third-party catalogue may be evaluated using the **e-sourcing capability model for service providers** (eSCM-SP™) developed by Carnegie Mellon University.

1.3.5 Service pipeline

The service pipeline consists of services under **development** for a given market space or **customer**. These services are to be phased into operation by service transition after completion of **design**, development, and testing. The pipeline represents the service provider's growth and strategic outlook for the future. The general health of the provider is reflected in the pipeline. It also reflects the extent to which new **service** concepts and ideas for improvement are being fed by **service strategy**, **service design** and continual improvement. Good **financial management** is necessary to ensure adequate funding for the pipeline.

1.3.6 Retired services

Some services in the catalogue are phased out or **retired**. Phasing out of services is part of **service transition**. This is to ensure that all commitments made to customers are duly fulfilled and **service assets** are released from **contracts**. When services are phased out, the related knowledge and information are stored in a knowledge base for future use. Phased-out services are not available to new customers or contracts unless a special **business case** is made. Such services may be reactivated into operations under special conditions and SLAs that are to be approved by senior management. This is necessary because such services may cost a lot more to support and may disrupt **economies of scale** and **scope**.

1.3.7 The role of service transition

Approval from **service transition** is necessary to add or remove services from the **service catalogue**. This is necessary for the following reasons:

- Once an item enters the catalogue it must be made available to customers who demand it. Due diligence is necessary to ensure that the service is a complete product that can be fully supported. This includes technical feasibility, financial viability, and operational **capability**. Incomplete products offered in haste can result in significant losses for service providers and customers.

- Items in the **service catalogue** are mostly in the **service operation** phase with contractual commitments made to customers. Any changes to the catalogue have to be evaluated for **impact** on the ability to meet those commitments.

- Adding items to the **service catalogue** means the need to set aside capabilities and **resources** for present and prospective customers. This is like maintaining spares for every piece of equipment in every type of aircraft in **operation** in the fleet. Having more has advantages if each item is doing well. Otherwise, valuable resources are locked by catalogue items not doing well. There is a need to balance flexibility and choice for customers with the increase in complexity, uncertainty, and resource conflicts.

There are instances in which certain **business** needs cannot be fulfilled with services from a catalogue. The **service provider** has to decide how to respond to such cases. The options are typically along the following lines:

- Explain to the **customer** why the need cannot be fulfilled.
- Explain what is needed of the customer in terms of commitment, sponsorship or funding for new service **development**. Customers may reconsider their needs in view of service development costs

they may have to bear.
  - Develop the service if the customer makes the necessary commitment
  - Decline the opportunity if the customer cannot commit.
- Consider supporting the customer in **partnership** with third parties.

1.3.8 Designing supporting systems, especially the service portfolio

The most effective way of managing all aspects of services through their **lifecycle** is by using appropriate **management systems** and tools to support and automate efficient processes. The **service portfolio** is the most critical management system used to support all processes and describes a provider's **services** in terms of business value. It articulates business needs and the provider's response to those needs. By definition, business value terms correspond to market terms, providing a means for comparing service competitiveness across alternative providers. By acting as the basis of a decision framework, a **service portfolio** either clarifies or helps to clarify the following **strategic** questions:

- Why should a **customer** buy these services?
- Why should they buy these services from you?
- What are the **pricing** or chargeback **models**?
- What are my strengths and weaknesses, priorities and **risk**?
- How should my **resources** and capabilities be allocated?

See Figure 1.4. Ideally the **service portfolio** should form part of a comprehensive service knowledge management system (SKMS) and registered as a **document** in the **configuration management system** (CMS). Further information is provided on both the CMS and the SKMS within the **Service Transition** publication. Figure 1.4 is a depiction of the relationship of the service portfolio with the SKMS.

Once a **strategic** decision to charter a service is made, this is the stage in the service lifecycle when **service design** begins architecting the service, which will eventually become part of the **service catalogue**. The **service portfolio** should contain information relating to every service and its current status within the **organization**. The options of **status** within the service portfolio

Figure 1.4 – The service portfolio – a central repository [4]

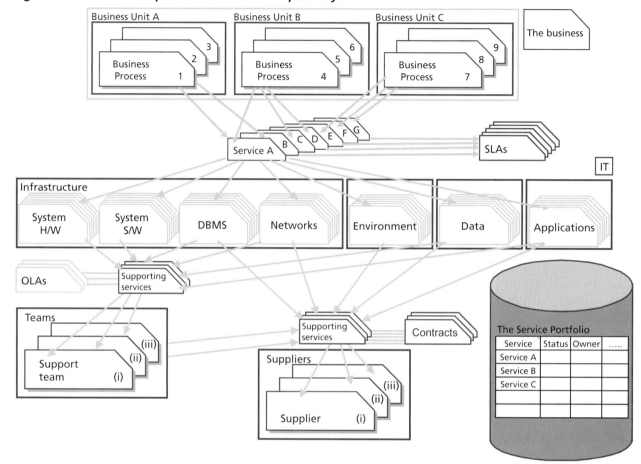

Source Service Design was produced by OGC

should include:

- **Requirements**: a set of outline requirements have been received from the business or IT for a new or changed service
- **Defined**: the set of requirements for the new service are being assessed, defined and documented and the SLR is being produced
- **Analysed**: the set of requirements for the new service are being analysed and prioritized
- **Approved**: the set of requirements for the new service have been finalized and authorized
- **Chartered**: the new service requirements are being communicated and resources and **budgets** allocated
- **Designed**: the new service and its constituent components are being designed – and procured, if required
- **Developed**: the service and its constituent **components** are being developed or harvested, if applicable
- **Built**: the service and its constituent components are being built

- **Test**: the **service** and its constituent components are being tested
- **Released**: the service and its constituent components are being released
- **Operational**: the service and its constituent components are operational within the **live environment**
- **Retired**: the service and its constituent components have been retired.

The **service portfolio** would therefore contain details of all services and their **status** with respect to the current stage within the service lifecycle, as illustrated in Figure 1.5.

Customers and **users** would only be allowed access to those services within the **service portfolio** that were of a **status** between 'chartered' and 'operational', as illustrated by the box in Figure 1.5, i.e. those services contained within the **service catalogue**. Service strategy and **service design** personnel would need access to all **records** within the service portfolio, as well as other important areas such as **change management**. Other members of the **service**

Figure 1.5 – The service portfolio and its contents [5]

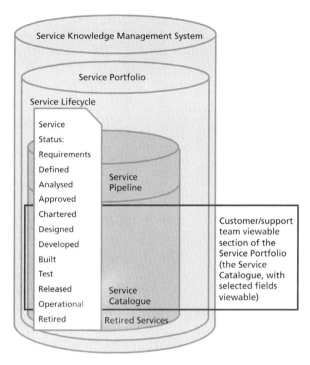

Source Service Design was produced by OGC

provider organization would have access to a permitted subset of the records within the service portfolio. Although the service portfolio is designed by service design, it is owned and managed by **service strategy** within the service portfolio management process. Full details on **service portfolio management** are discussed in the Service Strategy publication.

The service pipeline is a subset of the overall service portfolio and contains details of all of the business requirements that have not yet become services released to the **live environment**. It is used as a basis for the definition, analysis, prioritization and approval, by the ISG and service strategy, of all requests for new or changed services, to ensure that new and changed services are aligned to business requirements. It will principally be used as input to the activities of the service strategy and service design stages of the service lifecycle. It also provides valuable input to the activities of the **service transition** stage of the lifecycle in determining the services to be released. The service catalogue management process must ensure that all of the details within the **service portfolio** are accurate and up-to-date as the **requirement** and its new or changed service is migrated into the live environment. This will involve close liaison with all service transition activities.

Various elements of the same service can have different statuses at the same time. Otherwise the service portfolio would be unable to support 'incremental and iterative' **development**. Each organization should carefully design its service portfolio, the content and the access allowed to the content. The content should include:

- Service name
- Service description
- Service **status**
- Service **classification** and criticality
- **Applications** used
- Data and/or data schema used
- **Business process**es supported
- Business owners
- Business **users**
- IT owners
- **Service warranty** level, SLA and SLR references
- **Supporting services**
- Supporting **resources**
- Dependent **services**
- Supporting OLAs, **contracts** and **agreements**
- Service **costs**
- Service charges (if applicable)
- Service revenue (if applicable)
- Service **metrics**.

The **service portfolio** is the main source of information on the requirements and services and needs to be very carefully designed to meet all the needs of all its users. The **design** of the **service portfolio** needs to be considered in the same way as the design of any other **IT service** to ensure that it meets all of these needs. This approach should also be used for all of the other **service management** information systems, including the:

- Service knowledge management system (SKMS)
- **Configuration management (CMS)**
- Service desk system
- **Capacity management information system (CMIS)**
- **Availability management information system (AMIS)**
- Information security management system (ISMS)
- Supplier and contracts database (SCD).

Case example 1 (solution): *The lack of a service lifecycle*

The decision to adopt the **pricing strategy** did not appear to be coordinated with **service design**, service transition or **service operations**, indicating a lack of holistic or systems thinking in crafting the service **pricing** strategy. Though strategically sound, the pricing strategy did not consider the many interrelated parts of the entire system.

Among the unintended consequences is a **service strategy** that appeared in the front pages of world newspapers as a colossal blunder in **service management**.

SECTION 2 – PRINCIPLES RELATED TO SERVICE CATALOGUE

SCM:02

Understanding the terms related to ITIL v3 Service Catalogue Management enables one to begin to understand both the usefulness and worth that a well-executed Service Catalogue and Service Catalogue Management process can bring to a service provider and its customers and users.

The business services used day in and day out in business, government, education, healthcare, manufacturing, publishing – every type of business – are performances. IT systems spanning people, process, providers, products, and technology come together to facilitate the outcomes that customers and users desire. The composition of a service entwines provider and consumer inseparably. The Service Catalogue is not simply a static listing of available services. It is also much more than an automated method of requesting services. It is a means of seeing the entirety of IT service production and consumption.

A Service Catalogue provides interfaces for the providers, customers and users of IT services. Users gain access to automated fulfilment, information about the services they use. Customers gain visibility into which users are consuming how much of what, and at what cost. Providers learn how IT systems – themselves complex arrangements of people process and technology – combine to deliver value.

Whether providing services internally to an organization, externally to end-customers or some combination of both, the information that a Service Catalogue can produce is vitally important knowledge for both IT service provider and customer.

Delivering this capability requires careful planning and design of the Service Portfolio Management process technology that encapsulates the Service Catalogue and integrates it with other IT management and production systems. Done well, the Service Catalogue can provide tremendous guidance to assist with the design of new and changed services including the Service Portfolio itself, as well as the technology and related management systems, processes and management

metrics required. The Service Catalogue is truly the "spine" of ITIL v3, and careful planning is required to achieve the benefits it can provide.

This section serves to illustrate the value the Service Catalogue Management process can bring to an IT organization and, as a result, to the customers and users of the services it provides.

2.1 GOALS

The main goals and objectives of service design are to:

■ Design services to satisfy business objectives, based on the quality, compliance, risk and security requirements, delivering more effective and efficient IT and business solutions and services aligned to business needs by coordinating all design activities for IT services to ensure consistency and business focus

■ Design services that can be easily and efficiently developed and enhanced within appropriate timescales and costs and, wherever possible, reduce, minimize or constrain the long-term costs of service provision

■ Design efficient and effective processes for the design, transition, operation and improvement of high-quality IT services, together with the supporting tools, systems and information, especially the service portfolio, to manage services through their lifecycle

■ Identify and manage risks so that they can be removed or mitigated before services go live

■ Design secure and resilient IT infrastructures, environments, applications and data/ information resources and capability that meet the current and future needs of the business and customers

■ Design measurement methods and metrics for assessing the effectiveness and efficiency of the design processes and their deliverables

■ Produce and maintain IT plans, processes, policies, architectures, frameworks and documents for the design of quality IT solutions, to meet current and future agreed business needs

■ Assist in the development of policies and standards in all areas of design and planning of

IT services and processes, receiving and acting on feedback on design processes from all other areas and incorporating the actions into a continual process of improvement

■ Develop the skills and capability within IT by moving **strategy** and design activities into **operational** tasks, making effective and efficient use of all IT service resources

■ Contribute to the improvement of the overall quality of IT service within the imposed design constraints, especially by reducing the need for reworking and enhancing **services** once they have been implemented in the live environment.

2.1.1 Balanced design

For any new business requirements, the **design** of services is a delicate balancing act, ensuring that not only the functional requirements but also the **performance** targets are met. All of this needs to be balanced with regard to the resources available within the required timescale and the **costs** for the new services. Jim McCarthy, author of *Dynamics of Software Development*, states: 'As a development manager, you are working with only three things':

■ **Functionality**: the service or product and its facilities, functionality and **quality**, including all of the management and operational functionality required

■ **Resources**: the people, technology and money available

■ **Schedule**: the timescales.

2.1.2 Project elements in a triangulated relationship

This concept is extremely important to **service design** activities and to the balance between the effort that is spent in the design, **development** and delivery of services in response to business requirements. **Service design** is a delicate balancing act of all three elements and the constant dynamic adjustment of all three to meet changing business needs. Changing one side of the triangle invariably has an impact on at least one of the other sides if not both of them. It is vital therefore that the business drivers and needs are fully understood in order that the most effective business solutions are designed and delivered, using the most appropriate balance of these three elements. It is likely that business drivers and needs will change during design and delivery, due to market pressures. The functionality and resources should be considered for all stages of the service lifecycle, so that services are not only designed and developed effectively and efficiently, but that the **effectiveness** and **efficiency** of the service is maintained throughout all stages of its lifecycle.

Due consideration should be given within service design to all subsequent stages within the service lifecycle. Often designers and architects only consider the development of a new **service** up to the time of implementation of the service into the **live environment**. A holistic approach to the design of IT services should be adopted to ensure that a fully comprehensive and integrated solution is designed to meet the agreed requirements of the **business**. This approach should also ensure that all of the necessary mechanisms and functionality are implemented within the new service so that it can be effectively managed and improved throughout its operational life to achieve all of its agreed service targets. A formal, structured approach should be adopted to ensure that all aspects of the service are addressed and ensure its smooth introduction and **operation** within the live environment.

The most effective **IT service providers** integrate all five aspects of design rather than design them in isolation. This ensures that an integrated enterprise architecture is produced, consisting of a set of standards, designs and **architectures** that satisfy all of the management and **operational** requirements of services as well as the functionality required by the business. This integrated design ensures that when a new or changed service is implemented, it not only provides the functionality required by the business, but also meets and continues to meet all its **service levels** and targets in all areas. This ensures that no (or absolute minimum) weaknesses will need to be addressed retrospectively.

In order to achieve this, the overall management of these design activities needs to ensure:

■ Good communication between the various design activities and all other parties, including the business and IT planners and strategists

■ The latest **versions** of all appropriate business

and IT plans and strategies are available to all designers

■ All of the architectural documents and design documents are consistent with all business and IT policies and plans

■ The **architectures** and designs:

■ Are flexible and enable IT to respond quickly to new business needs

■ Integrate with all strategies and policies

■ Support the needs of other stages of the service lifecycle

■ Facilitate new or changed quality services and solutions, aligned to the needs and timescales of the **business**.

2.2 IDENTIFYING SERVICE REQUIREMENTS

Service design must consider all elements of the service by taking a holistic approach to the **design** of a new service. This approach should consider the service and its constituent **components** and their inter-relationships, ensuring that the services delivered meet the functionality and **quality** of service expected by the business in all areas:

■ The **scalability** of the service to meet future requirements, in support of the long-term **business objectives**

■ The **business processes** and **business units** supported by the service

■ The **IT service** and the agreed business functionality and requirements

■ The service itself and its **service level requirement (SLR)** or **service level agreement (SLA)**

■ The technology components used to deploy and deliver the service, including the infrastructure, the environment, the data and the **applications**

■ The internally supported **services** and components and their associated **operational level agreements (OLAs)**

■ The externally supported services and components and their associated **underpinning contracts**, which will often have their own related **agreements** and/or schedules

■ The **performance** measurements and metrics required

■ The legislated or required security levels.

The **relationships** and dependencies between

Figure 2.1 – The service relationships and dependencies

[6]

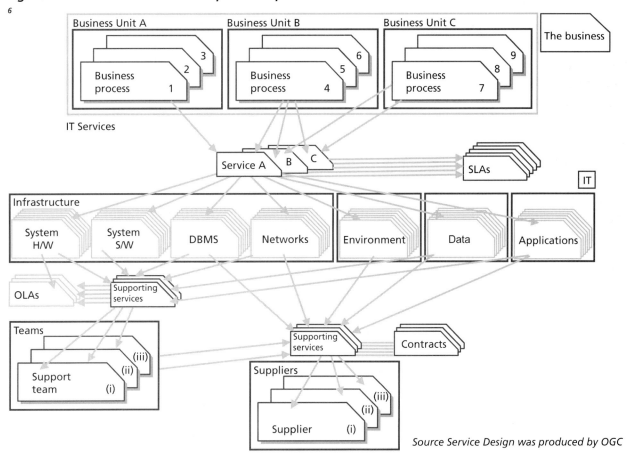

Source Service Design was produced by OGC

these elements are illustrated in Figure 2.1.

No service can be designed, transitioned and operated in isolation. The relationship of each service to its supporting **components** and services must be clearly understood and recognized by all people within the **service provider organization**. It is also essential that all targets contained within supporting **agreements**, such as OLAs and **contracts**, underpin those agreed between the **service provider** and its **customers**. Some of these concepts are discussed in more detail in later sections of the ITIL v3 Service Design book, with respect to the individual aspects of **service design**. However, when an individual aspect of a service is changed, all other areas of the service should also be considered to ensure that any amendments necessary to support the **change** are included in the overall design. Increasingly, services are complex and are delivered by a number of partner or **supplier** organizations. Where multiple **service providers** are involved in delivery of a service, it is vital that a central **service design** authority is established, to ensure services and **processes** are fully integrated across all parties.

Within the specific area of technology there are four separate technology domains that will need to be addressed, as they are the supporting components of every service and contribute to its overall performance:

- **Infrastructure**: the management and **control** of all infrastructure elements, including mainframes, **servers**, network equipment, database systems, storage area networks (SANs), network attached storage (NAS), systems software, utilities, **backup** systems, firewalls, **development** and **test** environments, management tools, etc.

- **Environmental**: the management and control of all environmental aspects of all major equipment rooms, including the physical space and layout, power, air conditioning, cabling, physical **security**, etc.

- **Data**: the management and control of all data and information and its associated access, including test data where applicable

- **Applications**: the management and control of all applications software, including both bought-in applications and in-house developed applications software.

2.2.1 Identifying and documenting business requirements and drivers

IT must retain accurate information on business requirements and drivers if it is to provide the most appropriate catalogue of services with an acceptable level of **service** quality that is aligned to business needs. Business drivers are the people, information and tasks that support the **fulfilment** of business objectives. This requires that IT develops and maintains close, regular and appropriate relationships and exchange of information in order to understand the **operational**, **tactical** and **strategic** requirements of the **business**. This information needs to be obtained and agreed in two main areas to maintain service alignment:

- **Information on the requirements of existing services** – what changes will be required to existing services with regard to:
  - New facilities and functionality requirements
  - Changes in **business processes**, dependencies, priorities, criticality and **impact**
  - Changes in volumes of service **transactions**
  - Increased **service levels** and **service level targets** due to new business driver, or reduced for old services, lowering priority for those due for replacement
  - Additional needs for **service management** information.

- **Information on the requirements of new services:**
  - Facilities and functionality required
  - **Management information** required and management needs
  - Business processes supported, dependencies, priorities, criticality and impact
  - Business cycles and seasonal variations
  - **Service level requirements** and **service level targets**
  - Business **transaction** levels, service transaction levels, numbers and types of **users** and anticipated future growth
  - Business justification, including the financial and **strategic** aspects
  - Predicted level of **change**, e.g. known future business requirements or enhancement
  - Level of business **capability** or support to be provided, e.g. local business-based support.

This collection of information is the first and most important stage for designing and delivering new services or major changes to existing services. The need for accurate and representative information from the **business** is paramount. This must be agreed and signed off with senior representatives within the business. If incorrect or misleading information is obtained and used at this stage, then all subsequent stages will be delivering services that do not match the needs of the business. Also, there must be some formal **process** for the agreement and acceptance of changes to the business requirements, as these will often change and evolve during the service lifecycle. The requirements and the **design** must evolve with the changing business **environment** to ensure that the business expectations are met. However, this must be a carefully managed process to ensure that the rate of change is kept at an agreed and manageable level, and does not 'swamp' and excessively delay the **project** or its implementation.

In order to design and deliver **IT services** that meet the needs of the customers and the business, clear, concise, unambiguous **specifications** of the requirements must be documented and agreed. Time spent in these activities will prevent issues and discussion from arising later with regard to **variances** from customer and business expectation. This business requirements stage should consist of:

- Appointment of a project manager, the creation of a project team and the agreement of project **governance** by the application of a formal, structured project methodology
- Identification of all stakeholders, including the documentation of all requirements from all stakeholders and **stakeholder** benefits they will obtain from the implementation
- Requirements analysis, prioritization, agreement and documentation
- Determination and agreement of outline **budgets** and business benefits. The budget must be committed by management, because it is normal **practice** to decide next year's budget in the last quarter of the previous year, so any plans must be submitted within this cycle
- Resolution of the potential conflict between **business units** and agreement on corporate requirements

- Sign-off processes for the agreed requirements and a method for agreeing and accepting changes to the agreed requirements. Often the process of developing requirements is an iterative or incremental approach that needs to be carefully controlled to manage '**scope** creep'
- Development of a customer engagement **plan**, outlining the main **relationships** between IT and the **business** and how these relationships and necessary communication to wider **stakeholders** will be managed.

Where service requirements are concerned, they sometimes come with a price tag (which might not be entirely known at this stage), so there always needs to be a balance between the **service** achievable and the **cost**. This may mean that some requirements may be too costly to include and may have to be dropped during the financial **assessment** involved within the **design** process. If this is necessary, all decisions to omit any service requirements from the design of the service must be documented and agreed with the representatives of the business. There is often a difficulty when what the business wants and the **budget** allocated for the solution do not take into account the full service costs, including the ongoing costs.

2.3 THE FOUR P'S OF SERVICE DESIGN

Many designs, plans and projects fail through a lack of preparation and management. The implementation of ITIL Service Management as a practice is about preparing and planning the effective and efficient use of the four Ps: the People, the Processes, the Products (services, technology and tools) and the Partners (suppliers, manufacturers and vendors),

2.4 SERVICE PROVIDER TYPES

'There is no such thing as a service industry. There are only industries whose service components are greater or less than those of other industries. Everybody is in service.'
Professor Emeritus Theodore Levitt, Harvard Business School

Case study 2: Infrastructure services
Some time in the late 1990s, the internal IT service provider for a global conglomerate decided to source all data centre operations to external service providers. The primary driver was lower costs. Five years and several mergers and acquisitions later, and despite having achieved its cost reductions, the internal provider is considering in-sourcing all data centre operations. What do you suspect is the reason?
(Answer at the end of the chapter)

It is necessary to distinguish between different types of service providers. While most aspects of service management apply equally to all types of service providers, others such as customers, contracts, competition, market spaces, revenue and strategy take on different meanings depending on the type. There are three archetypes of business models service providers:

■ Type I – internal service provider

■ Type II – shared services unit

■ Type III – external service provider

2.4.1 Type I (internal service provider)
Type I providers are typically business functions embedded within the business units they serve. The business units themselves may be part of a larger enterprise or parent organization. Business functions such as finance, administration, logistics, human resources, and IT provide services required by various parts of the business. They are funded by overheads and are required to operate strictly

within the mandates of the business. Type I providers have the benefit of tight coupling with their owner-customers, avoiding certain costs and risks associated with conducting business with external parties.

The primary objectives of Type I providers are to achieve functional excellence and cost-effectiveness for their business units. They specialize to serve a relatively narrow set of business needs. Services can be highly customized and resources are dedicated to provide relatively high service levels. The governance and administration of business functions are relatively straightforward. The decision rights are restricted in terms of strategies and operating models. The general managers of business units make all key decisions such as the portfolio of services to offer, the investments in capabilities and resources, and the metrics for measuring performance and outcomes.

Type I providers operate within internal market spaces. Their growth is limited by the growth of the business unit they belong to. Each business unit (BU) may have its own Type I provider (Figure 2.2). The success of Type I providers is not measured in terms of revenues or profits because they tend to operate on a cost-recovery basis with internal funding. All costs are borne by the owning business unit or enterprise.

Competition for Type I providers is from providers outside the business unit, such as corporate business functions, who wield advantages such as scale, scope, and autonomy. In general, service

Figure 2.2 – Type I providers [7]

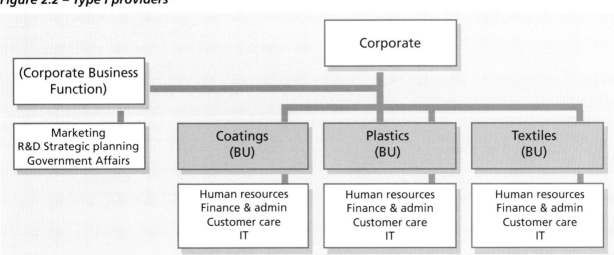

Source Service Strategy was produced by OGC

providers serving more than one customer face much lower risk of market failure. With multiple sources of demand, peak demand from one source can be offset by low demand from another. There is duplication and waste when Type I providers are replicated within the enterprise.

To leverage **economies of scale** and scope, Type I providers are often consolidated into a corporate business function when there is a high degree of similarity in their capabilities and resources. At this level of aggregation Type I providers balance enterprise needs with those at the business unit level. The trade-offs can be complex and require a significant amount of attention and **control** by senior executives. As such, consolidated Type I providers are more appropriate where classes of assets such as IT, R&D, marketing or manufacturing are at the core of the **organization**'s competitive advantage and therefore need careful control.

2.4.2   Type II (shared services unit)

Functions such as finance, IT, human **resources**, and logistics are not always at the core of an organization's competitive advantage. Hence, they need not be maintained at the corporate level where they demand the attention of the chief executive's team. Instead, the services of such shared functions are consolidated into an autonomous special unit called a shared services unit (SSU) (Figure 2.3). This **model** allows a more devolved governing structure under which SSU can focus on serving business units as direct customers. SSU can create, grow, and sustain an internal market for their services and model themselves along the lines of **service providers** in the open market. Like corporate **business** functions, they can leverage opportunities across the enterprise and spread their costs and **risks** across a wider base. Unlike corporate business functions, they have fewer protections under the banner of **strategic** value and core competence.

Figure 2.3 – Common Type II providers [8]

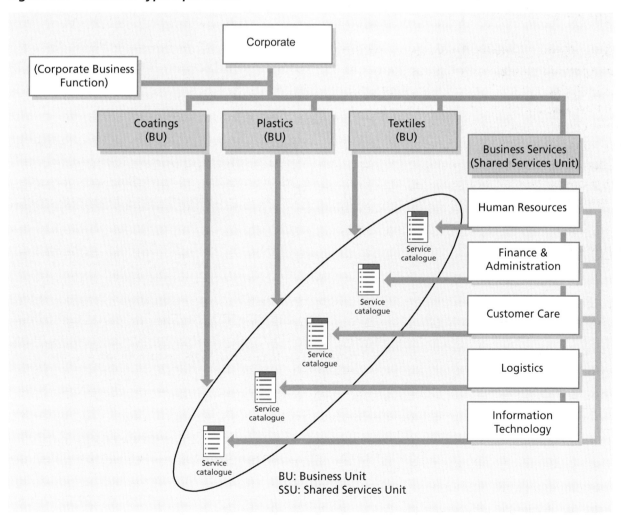

BU: Business Unit
SSU: Shared Services Unit

Source Service Strategy was produced by OGC

They are subject to comparisons with **external service providers** whose business practices, operating models and strategies they must emulate and whose **performance** they should approximate if not exceed. **Performance** gaps are justified through benefits received through services within their domain of control.

Customers of Type II are business units under a corporate parent, common stakeholders, and an enterprise-level **strategy**. What may be sub-optimal for a particular business unit may be justified by advantages reaped at the corporate level for which the business unit may be compensated. Type II can offer lower prices compared to external service providers by leveraging corporate advantage, internal **agreements** and **accounting** policies. With the autonomy to function like a business unit, Type II providers can make decisions outside the constraints of business unit level policies. They can standardize their service offerings across business units and use market-based pricing to influence demand patterns.

2.4.2.1 Market-based pricing

With market-based pricing there is minimal need for complex discussions and negotiations over specific **requirements**, technologies, resource allocations, **architectures**, and designs (that would be necessary with Type I arrangements) because the prices would drive adjustments, self-corrections and optimization on both sides of the value equation.

While Type II providers benefit from a relatively captive internal market for their services, their customers may still evaluate them in comparison with external service providers. This balance is crucial to the **effectiveness** of the shared services model. It also means that poorly performing Type II providers face the **threat** of substitution. This puts pressure on the leadership to adopt industry best practices, cultivate **market spaces**, formulate business strategies, strive for **operational effectiveness**, and develop distinctive capabilities. Industry-leading shared services units have successfully been spun off by their parents as independent **businesses** competing in the external market. They become a source of revenues from the initial charter of simply providing a **cost** advantage.

2.4.3 Type III (external service provider)

The business strategies of customers sometimes require capabilities readily available from a Type III provider. The additional **risks** that Type III providers assume over Type I and Type II are justified by increased flexibility and freedom to pursue opportunities. Type III providers can offer competitive prices and drive down **unit costs** by consolidating demand. Certain business strategies are not adequately served by **internal service providers** such as Type I and Type II. **Customers** may pursue sourcing strategies requiring services from external providers. The motivation may be access to knowledge, experience, scale, **scope**, capabilities, and resources that are either beyond the reach of the **organization** or outside the scope of a carefully considered investment portfolio. Business strategies often require reductions in the **asset base**, **fixed costs**, **operational** risks, or the redeployment of financial assets. Competitive business **environments** often require customers to have flexible and lean structures. In such cases it is better to buy services rather than own and **operate** the assets necessary to execute certain **business functions** and processes. For such customers, Type III is the best choice for a given set of services (Figure 2.4). The experience of such providers is not limited to any one enterprise or market. The breadth and depth of such experience is often the single most distinctive source of value for customers. The breadth comes from serving multiple types of customers or markets. The depth comes from serving multiples of the same type.

From a certain perspective, Type III providers are operating under an extended large-scale shared services **model**. They assume a greater level of risk from their customers compared to Type I and Type II. But their capabilities and **resources** are shared by their customers – some of whom may be rivals. This means that rival customers have access to the same bundle of assets, thereby diminishing any competitive advantage those assets bestowed.

Security is always an issue in shared services environments. But when the environment is shared with competitors, security becomes a larger concern. This is a **driver** of additional costs for Type III providers. As a counter-balance, Type III providers mitigate a type of risk inherent to Types

Figure 2.4 – Type III providers [9]

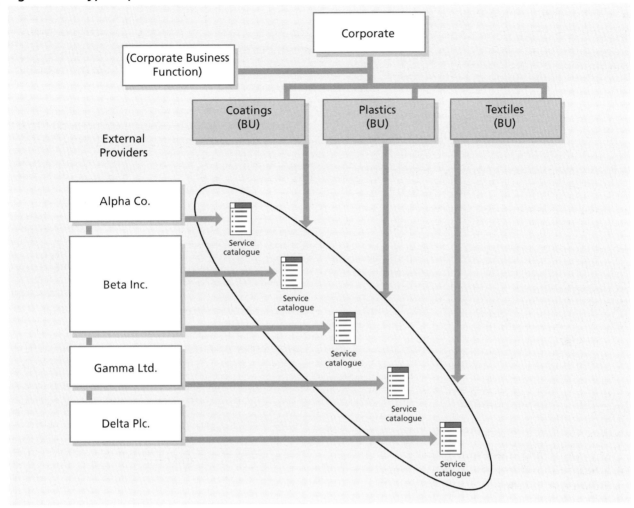

Source Service Strategy was produced by OGC

I and II: **business** functions and shared service units are subject to the same **system** of risks as their **business unit** or enterprise parent. This sets up a vicious cycle, whereby risks faced by the business units or the enterprise are transferred to the service units and then fed back with amplification through the services utilized. Customers may reduce systemic risks by transferring them to **external service providers** who spread those risks across a larger **value network**.

2.4.4 How do customers choose between types?

From a customer's perspective there are merits and demerits with each type of provider. **Services** may be sourced from each type of **service provider** with decisions based on **transaction** costs, strategic industry factors, core competence, and the **risk management** capabilities of the **customer**. The principles of specialization and coordination costs apply.

The principle of transaction costs is useful for

explaining why customers may prefer one type of provider to another. Transaction costs are overall costs of conducting a **business** with a service provider. Over and above the purchasing cost of services sold, they include but are not limited to the cost of finding and selecting qualified providers, defining **requirements**, negotiating **agreements**, measuring **performance**, managing the **relationship** with **suppliers**, cost of resolving disputes, and making changes or amends to agreements.

Additionally, whether customers keep a business **activity** in-house (aggregate) or decide to source it from outside (disaggregate) depends on answers to the following questions.

- Does the activity require **assets** that are highly specialized? Will those assets be idle or obsolete if that activity is no longer performed? (If yes, then disaggregate.)

- How frequently is the activity performed within a period or business cycle? Is it infrequent or sporadic? (If yes then disaggregate.)

■ How complex is the activity? Is it simple and routine? Is it stable over time with few changes? (If yes, then disaggregate.)

■ Is it hard to define good **performance**? (If yes, then aggregate.)

■ Is it hard to measure good performance? (If yes, then aggregate.)

■ Is it tightly coupled with other activities or assets in the business? Would separating it increase complexity and cause problems of coordination? (If yes, then aggregate.)

Based on the answers to those questions, customers may decide to switch between types of service providers. Answers to the questions themselves may change over time depending on new economic conditions, regulations, and technological innovation. **Transaction** costs are discussed further under the topics of **strategy**, tactics and operations, **service** structures and challenges and opportunities.

2.4.5 Customer decisions on service provider types

Customers may adopt a sourcing **strategy** that combines the advantages and mitigates the risks of all three types. In such cases, the **value network** supporting a **customer** cuts across the boundaries of more than one **organization**. As part of a carefully considered sourcing strategy, customers may allocate their needs across the different types of **service providers** based on whichever type best provides the **business** outcomes they desire. **Core services** are sought from Type I or Type II providers, while supplementary services enhancing core services are sought from Type II or Type III providers.

In a multi-sourced **environment**, the centre of gravity of a value network rests with the type of service provider dominating the sourcing portfolio. **Outsourcing** or disaggregating decisions move the centre of gravity away from corporate core. Aggregation or in-sourcing decisions move the centre of gravity closer to the corporate core and are driven by the need to maintain firm-specific advantages unavailable to competitors. Certain decisions do not shift the centre of gravity but rather reallocate services between service units of the same type.

The sourcing structure may be altered due to changes in the business fundamentals of the customer, making one type of service provider more desirable than the other. For example, a customer merger or acquisition may dramatically alter the economics that underpin a hitherto sound sourcing strategy. The customer decides to in-source an entire portfolio of services now to be offered by a newly acquired Type I or Type II.

2.4.5.1 The relative advantage of incumbency

Lasting relationships with customers allow organizations to learn and improve. Fewer **errors** are made, investments are recovered, and the resulting **cost** advantage can be leveraged to increase the gap with competition.

2.4.5.2 Advantage of being a well-performing incumbent

Customers find it less attractive to turn away from well-performing incumbents because of switching costs. Experience can be used to improve **assets** such as processes, knowledge, and the competencies that are **strategic** in nature.

Service providers must therefore focus on providing the basis for a lasting **relationship** with customers. It requires them to exercise strategic **planning** and **control** to ensure that common **objectives** drive everything, knowledge is shared effectively between units, and experience is fed back into future **plans** and actions for a steeper learning curve.

2.5 POLICIES, PRINCIPLES AND BASIC CONCEPTS

Over the years, organizations' **IT infrastructures** have grown and developed, and there may not be a clear picture of all the services currently being provided and the customers of each service. In order to establish an accurate picture, it is recommended that an IT service portfolio containing a **service catalogue** is produced and maintained to provide a central, accurate set of information on all services and to develop a service-focused **culture**.

The service portfolio should contain all the future requirements for services and the service catalogue should contain details of all services currently being provided or those being prepared for **transition** to the live environment, a summary of their characteristics, and details of the customers and maintainers of each. A degree of 'detective work' may be needed to compile this list and agree it with the customers (sifting through old documentation, searching program libraries, talking with IT staff and customers, looking at procurement **records** and talking with **suppliers** and contractors etc.). If a CMS or any sort of asset database exists, these may provide valuable sources of information, although they should be verified before inclusion within either the service portfolio or service catalogue. The **service portfolio** is produced as part of **service strategy** and should include participation by those involved in service design, transition, operation and improvement. Once a service is 'chartered' (being developed for use by customers, **service design** produces the specifications for the service and it is at this point that the service should be added to the service catalogue.

Each organization should develop and maintain a **policy** with regard to both the portfolio and the catalogue, relating to the services recorded within them, what details are recorded and what statuses are recorded for each of the services. The policy should also contain details of responsibilities for each section of the overall service portfolio and the **scope** of each of the constituent sections.

The service catalogue management process produces and maintains the service catalogue, ensuring that a central, accurate and consistent source of data is provided, recording the **status** of all **operational** services or services being transitioned to the **live environment**, together with appropriate details of each service. What is a service? This question is not as easy to answer as it may first appear, and many organizations have failed to come up with a clear definition in an IT context. IT staff often confuse a 'service' as perceived by the customer with an IT system. In many cases one 'service' can be made up of other 'services' (and so on), which are themselves made up of one or more IT systems within an overall infrastructure including hardware, software, networks, together with environments, data and **applications**. A good starting point is often to ask customers which IT services they use and how those services map onto and support their **business processes**. Customers

often have a greater clarity of what they believe a service to be. Each organization needs to develop a policy of what is a service and how it is defined and agreed within their own organization.

To avoid confusion, it may be a good idea to define a hierarchy of services within the **service catalogue**, by qualifying exactly what type of service is recorded, e.g. **business service** (that which is seen by the customer). Alternatively, **supporting services**, such as **infrastructure services**, network services, application services (all invisible to the customer, but essential to the delivery of IT services) will also need to be recorded. This often gives rise to a hierarchy of services incorporating customer services and other related services, including supporting services, shared services and commodity services, each with defined and agreed **service levels**.

When initially completed, the service catalogue may consist of a matrix, table or spreadsheet. Many organizations integrate and maintain their **service portfolio** and service catalogue as part of their CMS. By defining each service as a **configuration item** (CI) and, where appropriate, relating these to form a service hierarchy, the **organization** is able to relate events such as incidents and RFCs to the services affected, thus providing the basis for service **monitoring** and reporting using an integrated tool (e.g. 'list or give the number of incidents affecting this particular service'). It is therefore essential that changes within the service portfolio and service catalogue are subject to the **change management** process.

The service catalogue can also be used for other **service management** purposes (e.g. for performing a **business impact analysis** (BIA) as part of IT service continuity **planning**, or as a starting place for re-distributing **workloads**, as part of **capacity management**). The **cost** and effort of producing and maintaining the catalogue, with its **relationships** to the underpinning technology **components**, is therefore easily justifiable. If done in conjunction with prioritization of the BIA, then it is possible to ensure that the most important services are covered first. An example of a simple **service catalogue** that can be used as a starting point is given in Appendix G.

The **service catalogue** has two aspects:

- **The business service catalogue**: containing details of all the IT services delivered to the **customer**, together with relationships to the **business units** and the business process that rely on the **IT services**. This is the customer view of the **service catalogue**.

- **The technical service catalogue**: containing details of all the IT services delivered to the customer, together with relationships to the supporting services, shared services, components and CIs necessary to support the provision of the service to the **business**. This should underpin the business service catalogue and not form part of the customer view.

The relationship between these two aspects is illustrated in Figure 2.5.

Some organizations only maintain either a business service catalogue or a technical service catalogue. The preferred situation adopted by the more mature organizations maintains both aspects within a single service catalogue, which is part of a totally integrated **service management** activity and **service portfolio**. More information on the **design** and contents of a service catalogue is contained in Appendix G. The business service catalogue facilitates the development of a much more proactive or even pre-emptive SLM process, allowing it to develop more into the field of

business service management. The **technical service catalogue** is extremely beneficial when constructing the relationship between services, SLAs, OLAs and other underpinning **agreements** and **components**, as it will identify the technology required to support a service and the **support group**(s) that support the components. The combination of a business service catalogue and a technical service catalogue is invaluable for quickly assessing the **impact** of incidents and **changes** on the **business**.

2.6 DESIGN ASPECTS

An overall, integrated approach should be adopted for the design activities documented in the previous section and should cover the **design** of:

- **Service** solutions, including all of the functional requirements, **resources** and capabilities needed and agreed

- **Service management** systems and tools, especially the **service portfolio** for the management and control of services through their **lifecycle**

- Technology **architectures** and management architectures and tools required to provide the services

- Processes needed to design, **transition**, **operate** and improve the services

Figure 2.5 – The business service catalogue and the technical service catalogue [10]

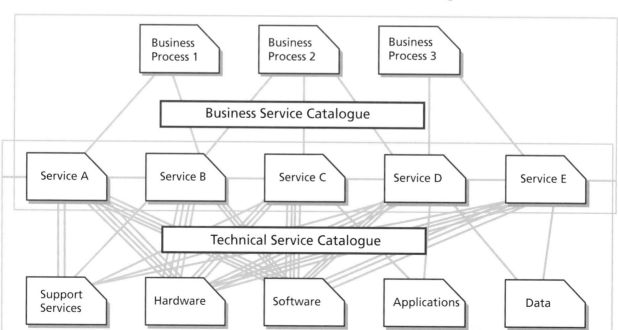

Source Service Design was produced by OGC

- Measurement systems, methods and **metrics** for the services, the architectures and their constituent **components** and the processes.

The key aspect is the design of new or changed service solutions to meet changing business needs. Every time a new service solution is produced, it needs to be checked against each of the other aspects to ensure that it will integrate and interface with all of the other **services** already in existence. The plans produced by service design for the design, **transition** and subsequent **operation** of these five different aspects should include:

- The approach taken and the associated timescales
- The organizational impact of the new or changed solution on both the **business** and IT
- The commercial impact of the solution on the **organization**, including the funding, **costs** and **budgets** required
- The technical impact of the solution and the staff and their **roles**, responsibilities, skills, knowledge, training and competences required to deploy, operate, maintain and **optimize** the new solution to the business
- The commercial justification **assessment** of the impact of the solution on existing business – this impact must be assessed from the point of view of IT and **service management** processes, including both their **capacity** and **performance**
- The assessment and mitigation of risks to services, **processes** and **service management** activities
- Communication **planning** and all aspects of communication with all interested parties
- The impact of the solution on new or existing **contracts** or **agreements**
- The expected **outcomes** from the operation of the new or changed service in measurable terms, generally expressed within new or existing **service level agreements** (SLAs), **service levels** and customer satisfaction
- The production of a **service design package** (see ITIL V3 Service Design book Appendix A) containing everything necessary for the subsequent testing, introduction and operation of the solution or service
- The production of a set of **service acceptance**

criteria (SAC) (see ITIL V3 Service Design book Appendix B) that will be used to ensure that the **service provider** is ready to deliver and support the new or changed service in the **live environment**.

2.6.1   Designing service solutions

There are many activities that have to be completed within the **service design** stage for a new or changed service. A formal and structured approach is required to produce the new service at the right cost, functionality, **quality** and within the right time frame. This process and its constituent stages are illustrated in Figure 2.6, together with the other major areas that will need to be involved within the process. This process must be iterative/incremental to ensure that the service delivered meets the evolving and changing needs of the **business** during the **business process** development and the IT service lifecycle. Additional project managers and project teams may need to be allocated to manage the stages within the **lifecycle** for the **deployment** of the new **service**.

The **role** of the project team within this activity of delivering new and changing **IT services** to the business and its **relationship** to design activities is illustrated in Figure 2.6 (see over).

Figure 2.6 shows the lifecycle of a service from the initial or changed business **requirement** through the **design**, **transition** and **operation** stages of the lifecycle. It is important that there is effective transfer of knowledge at all stages between the **operational** staff and the project staff to ensure smooth progression through each of the stages illustrated.

Case study 2 (solution): *Newly acquired service provider types*
The Type II provider for the conglomerate had achieved its cost reductions through a relationship with a Type III. As a result of mergers and acquisitions **activity**, however, the company grew to include additional Type I providers.

When the company re-examined its **service strategy**, it realized it could in-source and consolidate all service providers into a single Type II – at a lower cost and with an enhanced technological distinctiveness unavailable from any Type III.

Figure 2.6 – Aligning new services to business requirements [11]

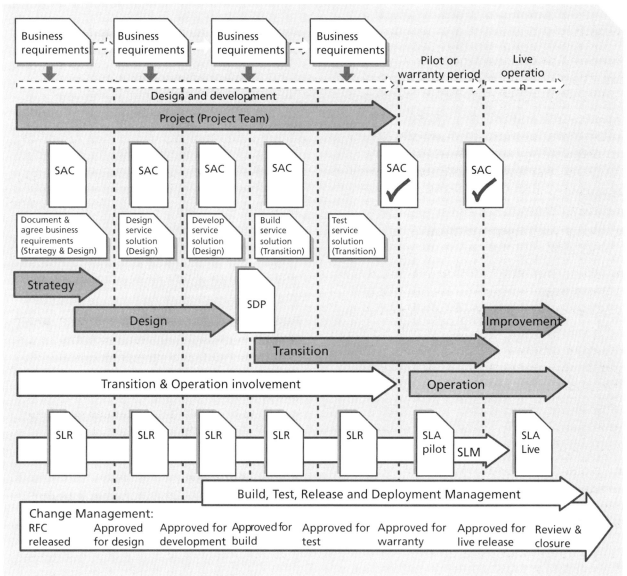

Source Service Design was produced by OGC

SECTION 3 – TECHNOLOGY FOR SERVICE CATALOGUE

SCM:03

A Service Catalogue is ultimately an IT service and, as such, requires technology to instantiate it and to deliver its value. There are many forms of Service Catalogue, depending on the objectives of its provider. Understanding the ways in which a Service Catalogue can interact with its many users, and what features it must provide, is of paramount importance to meeting successfully the objectives for which it is implemented.

As Information Technology becomes more widespread in society, people are becoming more comfortable with taking control of their personal IT service experiences. Many younger people have grown up with computers and the Internet. For them, resolving issues, researching options and requesting upgrades, installations, moves, adds or changes to service are second nature. These types of users prefer doing things on their own.

Technology has reached a point today where totally automated systems, such as those possible in a modern Service Catalogue solution, can and do provide faster, better and more desirable service than human-based options for an ever-increasing number of people.

Today's Service Catalogue solutions offer much more than statically-displayed service information or usage statistics. Modern Service Catalogue systems provide self-help, manage Request Fulfilment, diagnose Capacity issues, help manage Changes and provide IT-increased visibility into service production and delivery, helping optimize the efficiency and effectiveness of its delivery.

Understanding the capabilities of Service Catalogue technology, and understanding the various usage models and methods that a technical solution such as a Service Catalogue can allow, is very important to achieving a successful implementation. Choosing the right solution with the proper balance of features is vital to creating, managing and maintaining a Service Catalogue solution and thus obtaining the expected value.

This section explores the use of technology and tools that support Service Catalogue Management.

3.1 REQUEST FULFILMENT

Integrated ITSM technology is needed so that **service request**s can be linked to incidents or **event**s that have initiated them (and been stored in the same CMS, which can be interrogated to report against SLAs). Some organizations will be content to use the **incident management** element of such tools and to treat service requests as a subset and defined **category** of incidents. Where an **organization** chooses to raise separate service requests, it will require a tool which allows this **capability**.

Front-end self-help capabilities will be needed to allow users to submit requests via some form of web-based, menu-driven selection process. In all other respects the facilities needed to manage service requests are very similar to those for managing incidents: pre-defined workflow control of request models, **priority** levels, automated escalation, effective reporting, etc.

3.1.1 Request

The term '**service request**' is used as a generic description for many varying types of demands that are placed upon the IT department by the users. Many of these are actually small changes – low **risk**, frequently occurring, low **cost**, etc. (e.g. a request to change a password, a request to install an additional software **application** onto a particular workstation, a request to relocate some items of desktop equipment) or maybe just a question requesting information – but their scale and frequent, low-risk nature means that they are better handled by a separate **process**, rather than being allowed to congest and obstruct the normal incident and **change management** processes.

3.2 TYPES OF SERVICE TECHNOLOGY ENCOUNTERS

Advances in communication technologies are having a profound effect on the manner in which **service provider**s interact with customers. Airport kiosks, for example, have changed the interaction between airlines and their customers. There are four modes in which technology interacts with a

Figure 3.1 – Types of service technology encounters [12]

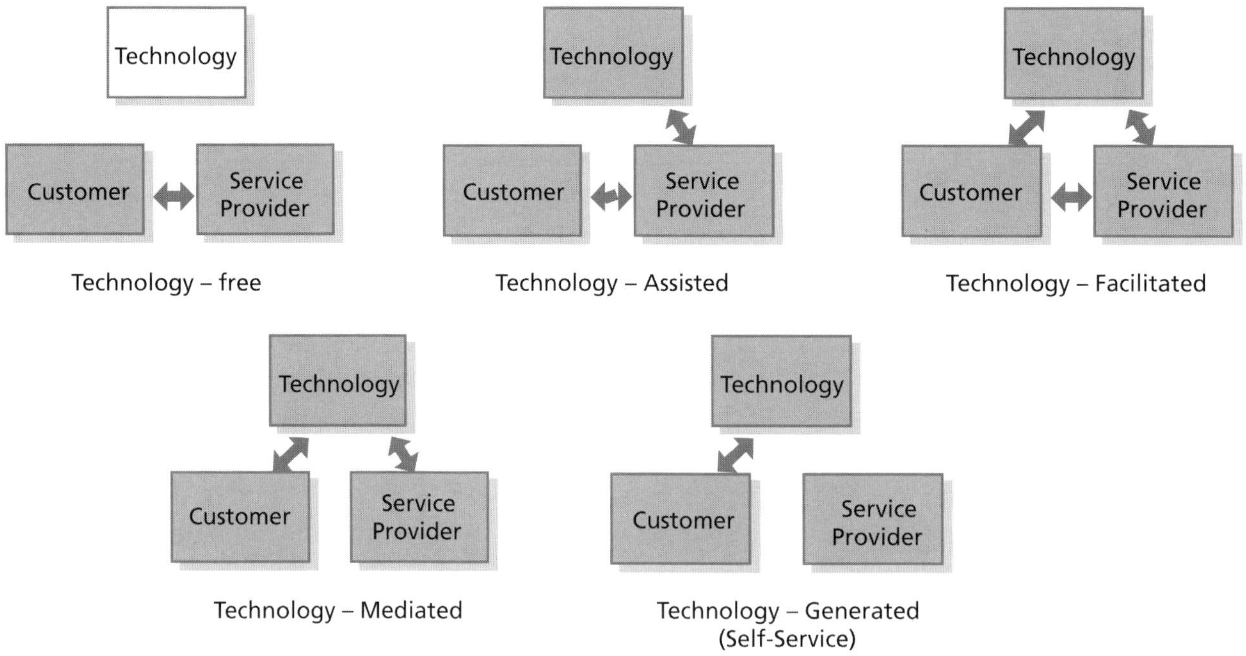

Technology – free

Technology – Assisted

Technology – Facilitated

Technology – Mediated

Technology – Generated
(Self-Service)

Source Service Strategy was produced by OGC

service provider's customers (Figure 3.1).

■ Mode A: technology-free – technology is not involved in the service encounter. Consulting services, for example, may be Mode A.

■ Mode B: technology-assisted – a service encounter where only the service provider has access to the technology. For example, an airline representative who uses a terminal to check in passengers is Mode B.

■ Mode C: technology-facilitated – a service encounter where both the service provider and the customer have access to the same technology. For example, a planner in consultation with a customer can refer to 'what if' scenarios on a personal computer to illustrate capacity and availability modelling profiles.

■ Mode D: technology-mediated – a service encounter where the service provider and the customer are not in physical proximity. Communication may be through a phone. For example, a customer who receives technical support services from a service desk is Mode D.

■ Mode E: technology-generated – a service encounter where the service provider is represented entirely by technology, commonly known as self-service. For example, bank ATMs, online banking and distance learning are Mode E.

Encounters should be designed while considering customer assets.

■ Are customer employees technical or non-technical?

■ What are the implications of the technology encounter to the customer?

■ What are the customer expectations and perceptions?

For example, Mode E may be less effective than Mode B or C in cases where the encounter is complex or ambiguous. When the encounter is routine and explicit, as in password resets, Mode E may be preferred. Other modes may have secondary considerations. Mode D, for example, may have language or time-zone implications.

3.3 SELF-SERVICE CHANNELS

Automation is useful to supplement the capacity of services. Self-service channels are increasingly popular among users now accustomed to human–computer interactions, devices and appliances. The ubiquitous channel of service delivery is the internet with browsers acting as service access points that are widely distributed, standardized and highly familiar through constant use. Advances in artificial intelligence and speech recognition have improved the capabilities of software-based service agents in conducting dialogue with customers. The richness of the dialogue and the complexity of the interaction continue to increase.

The capacity of self-service channels has very low marginal cost, is highly scalable, does not suffer from fatigue, offers highly consistent performance, and is offered on a 24/7 basis at a relatively low cost. Additionally, users perceive the following disadvantages with human-to-human interactions with respect to incidents and problems:

■ The emotional burden that the user is asked to carry in complaining about the service

■ Variability in the experience, competence and emotional state of human agents

■ Limited capacity of human resources, which causes uncertainty in wait times

■ The need to schedule certain interactions with staff

■ The fees associated with certain human resources.

Self-service channels are effective when appropriate knowledge and service logic is embedded into the self-service terminal. Service design should ensure that use case analysis is performed to ensure usability, efficiency and ease in interactions through the automated interface.

Another example would be the use of the productive capacity of customers through self-service channels. Advances in human-computer interaction and the richness of interaction technologies, such as touch-screens, scanners and signature capture devices, allow for certain service activities to be completed without the presence or intervention of service staff. This is a very intelligent way to adjust capacity that is highly sensitive to the presence of demand. Each customer brings one additional unit of productive capacity, instantly added and removed from the system without inventory-carrying costs to the service provider.

It is necessary to evaluate the level of control users are expected to assume with self-service options. The level of control should be commensurate with the proficiency and experience level of the users. In almost every population of users there are differences in levels of experience, skills, aptitudes and work

environments that determine preferences for methods and modes of interaction. The attributes and functions of service interfaces should take these differences into account. There will be trade-offs as different segments of users expect to be served according to their preferences. Some prefer step-by-step guidance while others prefer efficiency and flexibility. Advances in artificial intelligences and machine learning are creating a new level of sophistication for service interfaces, which are context-aware, forgiving of new users, and capable of dialogue embedded with inquiry. The principle of forgiveness requires that the design of a service helps users avoid errors. When the errors do occur, the design should minimize negative consequences.

3.4 IT SERVICE MANAGEMENT SUITES

The success of ITIL within the industry has encouraged software vendors to provide tools and suites of tools that are very compatible with the ITIL process framework providing significant levels of integration between the processes and their associated record types. This functionality creates a rich source of data and creates many of the inputs to CSI including:

■ **Incidents** that capture the service or the configuration item (CI) affected are a prime input to CSI enabling an understanding of the issues that are affecting the overall service provision and related support activities. Incident matching functionality allows the service desk to quickly relate like issues and create master records that highlight common situations that are affecting the users with associated resolution data to enhance problem identification and reduce the mean time to restore service (MTRS).

■ **Problems** are defined with integrated links to the associated incidents that confirmed their existence. Using the configuration data from the CMS to understand the relationships, problem management now has a source of related data to enable the root cause analysis process including change and release history of the affected CI or service.

■ **Changes** are often the first area of investigation following a service failure, again using the integration capabilities of the ITSM tool suite; it can be easier to trace

Figure 3.2 – Configuration management system [13]

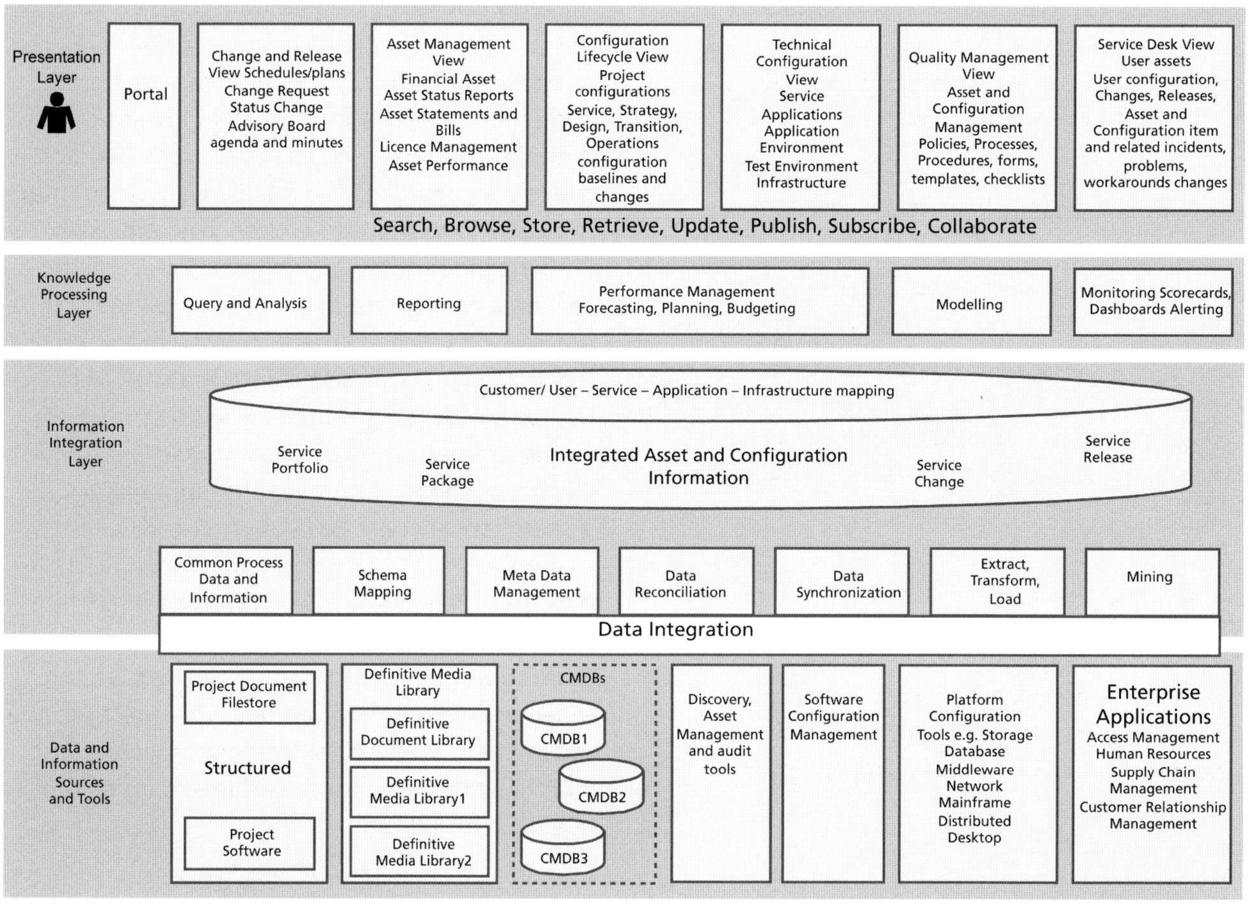

Source Continual Service Improvement was produced by OGC

the changes that have been made to a service or a CI. The **change schedule** and projected service outage (PSO) can be automated using calendaring capabilities to ensure visibility of changes and calculated impacts to the **service level agreements**. Recent improvements in the ITSM tools now allow for automated **risk assessment** and prioritization of changes, highlighting potential conflicts and reducing the administrative **overhead** for the **Change Advisory Board**.

Tool functionality in support of **configuration management** and the CMS has never been more advanced with extensive discovery and service **dependency** mapping capabilities. The CMS is the foundation for the integration of all ITSM tool functionality and is a critical data source for the CSI mission. While the **service provider** must still define the overall configuration management **process** and create the data **model** associated with their specific **environment**, the tools to establish and manage the CMS and the overall service delivery **architecture** have become very

powerful. Key functionality includes: discovery and reconciliation capabilities to capture CIs within the environment, visualization of the hierarchy and CI **relationships** for ease of understanding and support, **audit** tools to streamline the **verification** activities and the ability to federate data sources where appropriate.

The ability to coordinate releases and manage the contents of these releases are also more mature with native support for the definitive libraries and key integration points to the CMS and to specialized **version** control software packages. Functionality typically includes support for **release records** that consolidate and contain release contents enabling the attachment of related objects and **documents** pertaining to the release. Integration is normally provided to enable hyperlinking to the associated change records that are part of a release and the related **incident**, problem or **service request** records that were the catalyst for the original RFC. Release versions are also supported with predefined naming and numbering standards that enhance the understanding of the overall process. Overall reporting of release status and associated performance metrics are required as inputs to CSI ensuring that the deployment of new services are of the highest possible quality.

Service level management functionality is also well supported within the ITSM tool suites of today enabling the linkage of incidents, problems, changes and releases to associated service level management records such as SLAs, OLAs and UCs. Most tool suites support automated SLAM charts (service level agreement monitoring) highlighting which agreements are within tolerance, are threatened or have been broken. This automation is driven by the ability to define key SLA criteria and use related operational support records to trigger thresholds (e.g. a priority one incident is about to break the one-hour resolution target time or a change has caused a longer downtime than was agreed). CMS functionality can also support the concept of prioritized CIs that underpin specific service levels highlighting a greater impact if a failed component supports a critical service or business process. Some suites also provide the ability to trigger availability impacts to SLAs by capturing incident data related to service outages. Many of the suites also facilitate the definition of the service portfolio and the service catalogue while managing the workflow associated with the fulfilment of service requests. Some standalone point solutions support specialized functionality in this area (see below).

Reporting is one of the key benefits of an integrated ITSM suite with the ability to provide management information in a common format utilizing the combined data from all operational areas of the service lifecycle. This is of significant benefit enabling analysis of the relationships between service management events (e.g. incidents that result in problems, changes that cause incidents, releases that encapsulate certain changes) and all of the associated performance metric data that will feed the overall CSI initiatives.

3.4.1 Service request and fulfilment (service catalogue and workflow)

There are specialized tools that deal with service catalogue definition, request management and the workflow associated with the fulfilment of these requests. Some of these tools provide the workflow engines and some rely heavily on the capabilities of the companion ITSM suite. These tools provide the technology required to define the services within a catalogue structure in conjunction with the business customers and create a service portal (normally web-based) that allows users to request services. The request is then managed through the workflow engine assigning resources according to a defined process of tasks and related activities for each request type. These tools typically also capture related cost information to be fed to the financial systems for later charging activities. This functionality does much to support IT's integration with the business, defining services that underpin their mission and streamlining the delivery of commodity services that so often become a source of customer frustration. As in other tools, the true CSI benefit is the data that is collected and reported relate to the quality of the services delivered, any bottlenecks encountered, and the ability to track the achievement of related service levels.

3.4.2 Financial management

Financial management is a critical component of the IT services mission to ensure that there are enough financial resources to maintain and develop the IT infrastructure and professional capabilities in support of the current and future needs of the business. A balanced budget in IT through the recovery of IT costs, with a solid understanding of the fiscal aspects of their operations, will enable IT executives to justify their expenses in terms of the business services being supported.

In an increasing number of IT organizations this requires keeping track of resource and service utilization for the purpose of billing and chargeback of the shared IT resources. The costing and resource consumption measurement becomes critical to effectively and accurately charge business customers in an equitable, visible and auditable way.

Financial management tools collect raw metering data from a variety of sources including operating systems, databases, middleware and applications associating this usage to users of services from specific departments. Data collectors gather critical usage metrics for each of the technologies being measured, links in the costing information from accounting software and then reports, analyses and allocates costs, enabling customers to evaluate the information in many dimensions.

Most tools will interface with the CMS to manage costs for each CI and resource to generate data related to billing, reporting, chargeback and cost analysis. These tools will typically federate with the organization's financial management applications and ERP system to acquire and share aggregate costs. Interfaces are also normally supported with project and portfolio management tools to facilitate the overall portfolio of investments.

Effective cost management is a basic requirement for the IT organizations of today, financial management tools will be required to ensure that customers can not only understand the IT costs of their business operations, but also more accurately budget and enable IT to evaluate the overall effectiveness of the services provision. Successful implementation and usage of these tools will support the continual improvement of cost management and drive ever-increasing IT value to the business.

3.4.3 Business intelligence/reporting

In addition to the statistical analysis environment that requires a toolset to support technical data, there is also a need for a common repository of all service information and business-related data. Often these tools are provided by the same vendors who support the statistical analysis software but the focus in this instance is on providing business-related data from all of the above toolsets representing a guide to direct the activities of IT as a whole in support of the business customer.

As the technology used to deliver IT services becomes increasingly complex, the distribution of services expands and the amount of centralized control we can apply is diminished, there will be a growing reliance on tools and software functionality to administer, manage, improve and ensure overall governance of IT service provision. As stated earlier, best-practice process should determine what support functionality is required but we can be assured that the software industry will continue to develop a wide and varied set of tools that can reduce the administrative overhead of managing our processes and improve the overall quality of IT service provision.

SECTION 4 – A PROJECT PLAN APPROACH

SCM:04

Very often, when attempting to implement new technologies or processes, the difference between success and failure relates directly to understanding the current workflow and functional activities carried out. Approaching the creation of a Service Catalogue and the Service Catalogue Management process using such a project plan approach is one way to help assure success. Using formal project planning can prevent overlooking critical details.

The first step, therefore, in a project plan approach towards the creation of a Service Catalogue is understanding existing workflows, documentation, roles, and responsibilities. The new Service Catalogue will automate many of these items. Others, which perhaps are not encapsulated within the Service Catalogue, may need to change. Another very good place to begin understanding the needs for a Service Catalogue, as well as developing a project plan approach, is to examine what ITIL v3 refers to as the Service Design Package or SDP - the form requirements and specifications documentation which every organization that delivers IT services has. Before embarking on the creation of the Service Catalogue, it is critical to understand the types and forms of information that already exist within the organization and which will need to be incorporated in the Service Catalogue.. In addition, the Service Catalogue can perhaps indicate missing elements within the SDP.

In most organizations a Service Catalogue is either new or an enhancement to a more traditional static listing of services. In order to maximize the success of the Service Catalogue initiative one of the key aspects of the project plan needs to be the consideration of roles and responsibilities. There are unique requirements placed upon those who administer and maintain a Service Catalogue solution and, while the experience and expertise may exist in the organization, there are times when additional training and support is required.

Finally, a journey should begin with the end in mind. Understanding how a functional Service Catalogue may actually appear is very important.

Visualizing and perhaps even prototyping mockups of the service Catalogue and ensuring that models will meet expectations can be one of the final steps in the project plan approach.

This section explains the importance of using a project plan approach and methodology for the creation of a Service Catalogue.

4.1 PROCESS ACTIVITIES, METHODS AND TECHNIQUES

The key activities within the service catalogue management process should include:

■ Agreeing and documenting a service definition with all relevant parties

■ Interfacing with service portfolio management to agree the contents of the service portfolio and service catalogue

■ Producing and maintaining a service catalogue and its contents, in conjunction with the service portfolio

■ Interfacing with the business and IT service continuity management on the dependencies of business units and their business processes with the supporting IT services, contained within the business service catalogue

■ Interfacing with support teams, suppliers and configuration management on interfaces and dependencies between IT services and the supporting services, components and CIs contained within the technical service catalogue

■ Interfacing with business relationship management and service level management to ensure that the information is aligned to the business and business process.

4.1.1 The service design package

A 'service design package' or SDP should be produced during the design stage, for each new service, major change to a service or removal of a service or changes to the 'service design package' itself. This pack is then passed from service design to service transition and details all aspects of the service and its requirements through all of the subsequent stages of its lifecycle. The SDP should contain:

Table 4.1 – Contents of the service design package [14]

Category	Sub-category	Description of what is in the SDP
Requirements	Business requirements	The initial agreed and documented business requirements
	Service applicability	This defines how and where the service would be used. This could reference business, customer and user requirements for internal services
	Service contacts	The business contacts, customer contacts and stakeholders in the service
Service design	Service functional requirements	The changed functionality of the new or changed service, including its planned outcomes and deliverables, in a formally agreed statement of requirements (SoR)
	Service level requirements	The SLR, revised or new SLA, including service and quality targets
	Service and operational management requirements	Management requirements to manage the new or changed service and its components, including all supporting services and agreements, control, operation, monitoring, measuring and reporting
	Service design and topology	The design, transition and subsequent implementation and operation of the service solution and its supporting components, including: ■ The service definition and model, for transition and operation ■ All service components and infrastructure (including H/W, S/W, networks, environments, data, applications, technology, tools, documentation), including version numbers and relationships, preferably within the CMS ■ All user, business, service, component, transition, support and operational documentation ■ Processes, procedures, measurements, metrics and reports ■ Supporting products, services, agreements and suppliers
Organizational readiness assessment	Organizational readiness assessment	'Organizational readiness assessment' report and plan, including: business benefit, financial assessment, technical assessment, resource assessment and organizational assessment, together with details of all new skills, competences, capabilities required of the service provider organization, its suppliers, supporting services and contracts
Service lifecycle of plan	Service programme	An overall programme or plan covering all stages the lifecycle of the service, including the

		timescales and phasing, for the **transition**, **operation** and subsequent improvement of the new service including: ■ Management, coordination and integration with any other projects, or new or changed activities, services or processes ■ Management of risks and issues ■ Scope, objectives and components of the service ■ Skills, competences, roles and responsibilities ■ Processes required ■ Interfaces and dependencies with other services ■ Management of teams, resources, tools, technology, budgets, facilities required ■ Management of suppliers and contracts ■ Progress reports, reviews and revision of the programme and plans ■ Communication plans and training plans ■ Timescales, deliverables, targets and quality targets for each stage
	Service transition plan	Overall transition **strategy**, objectives, **policy**, **risk assessment** and plans including: ■ Build policy, plans and requirements, including service and component build plans, specifications, control and environments, technology, tools, processes, methods and mechanisms, including all platforms ■ Testing policy, plans and requirements, including test environments, technology, tools, processes, methods and mechanisms ■ Testing must include: 　■ Functional testing 　■ Component testing, including all suppliers, contracts and externally provided supporting products and services 　　User acceptance and usability testing 　■ System compatibility and integration testing 　■ Service and component performance and capacity testing 　■ Resilience and continuity testing 　■ Failure, alarm and event categorization, processing and testing 　■ Service and component, security and integrity testing 　■ Logistics, release and distribution testing 　■ Management testing, including **control**, monitoring, measuring and reporting, together with **backup**, recovery and all batch scheduling and processing ■ Deployment policy, **release** policy, plans and

		requirements, including logistics, deployment, roll-out, staging, deployment environments, cultural change, organizational change, technology, tools, processes, approach, methods and mechanisms, including all platforms, knowledge, skill and competence transfer and development, supplier and contract transition, data migration and conversion
	Service operational acceptance plan	Overall operational strategy, objectives, policy, risk assessment and plans including: ■ Interface and dependency management and planning ■ Events, reports, service issues, including all changes, releases, resolved incidents, problems and known errors, included within the service and any errors, issues or non-conformances within the new service ■ Final service acceptance
	Service acceptance criteria	Development and use of service acceptance criteria (SAC) for progression through each stage of the service lifecycle, including: ■ All environments ■ Guarantee and pilot criteria and periods

Source Service Strategy was produced by OGC

4.2 ROLES REQUIRED TO MANAGE THE SERVICE CATALOGUE

4.2.1 Process owner

A process owner is responsible for ensuring that their process is being performed according to the agreed and documented process and is meeting the aims of the process definition. This includes such tasks as:

■ Documenting and publicizing the process

■ Defining the key performance indicators (KPIs) to evaluate the effectiveness and efficiency of the process

■ Reviewing KPIs and taking action required following the analysis

■ Assisting with and being ultimately responsible for the process design

■ Improving the effectiveness and efficiency of the process

■ Reviewing any proposed enhancements to the process

■ Providing input to the ongoing service improvement plan

■ Addressing any issues with the running of the process

■ Ensuring all relevant staff have the required training in the process and are aware of their role in the process

■ Ensures that the process, roles, responsibilities and documentation are regularly reviewed and audited

■ Interfaces with line management, ensuring that the process receives the necessary staff resources. (Line management and process owners have complementary tasks – they need to work together to ensure efficient and effective processes. Often it is the task of line management to ensure the required training of staff.)

4.2.2 Service design manager

The key role and responsibilities of the service design manager are covered throughout this publication and they are responsible for the overall coordination and deployment of quality solution designs for services and processes.

Responsibilities of the role over and above those of line management of all people involved in service design roles include:

- Taking the overall service strategies and ensuring they are reflected in the service design practice and the service designs that are produced to meet and fulfil the documented business requirements
- Designing the functional aspects of the services as well as the infrastructure, environment applications and data management
- Producing quality, secure and resilient designs for new or improved services, technology architecture, processes or measurement systems that meet all the agreed current and future IT requirements of the organization
- Producing and maintaining all design documentation, including designs, plans, architectures and policies
- Producing and maintaining all necessary SDPs
- Measuring the effectiveness and efficiency of the service design process.

4.2.3 Service catalogue manager

The service catalogue manager has responsibility for producing and maintaining the service catalogue. This includes responsibilities such as:

- Ensuring that all operational services and all services being prepared for operational running are recorded within the service catalogue
- Ensuring that all the information within the service catalogue is accurate and up-to-date
- Ensuring that all the information within the service catalogue is consistent with the information within the service portfolio
- Ensuring that the information within the service catalogue is adequately protected and backed up.

4.2.4 Service level manager

The service level manager has responsibility for ensuring that the aims of service level management are met. This includes responsibilities such as:

- Keeping aware of changing business needs
- Ensuring that the current and future service requirements of customers are identified, understood and documented in SLA and SLR documents

- Negotiating and agreeing levels of service to be delivered with the customer (either internal or external); formally documenting these levels of service in SLAs
- Negotiating and agreeing OLAs and, in some cases, other SLAs and agreements that underpin the SLAs with the customers of the service
- Assisting with the production and maintenance of an accurate service portfolio, service catalogue, application portfolio and the corresponding maintenance procedures
- Ensuring that targets agreed within underpinning contracts are aligned with SLA and SLR targets
- Ensuring that service reports are produced for each customer service and that breaches of SLA targets are highlighted, investigated and actions taken to prevent their recurrence
- Ensuring that service performance reviews are scheduled, carried out with customers regularly and are documented with agreed actions progressed
- Ensuring that improvement initiatives identified in service reviews are acted on and progress reports are provided to customers
- Reviewing service scope, SLAs, OLAs and other agreements on a regular basis, ideally at least annually
- Ensuring that all changes are assessed for their impact on service levels, including SLAs, OLAs and underpinning contracts, including attendance at CAB meetings if appropriate
- Identifying all key stakeholders and customers
- Developing relationships and communication with stakeholders, customers and key users
- Defining and agreeing complaints and their recording, management, escalation, where necessary, and resolution
- Definition recording and communication of all complaints
- Measuring, recording, analysing and improving customer satisfaction.

4.2.5 What is the vision?

The starting point for all of these activities is the culture and environment of the service provider organization. The people and the culture have to be appropriate and acceptable to improvement and change. Therefore, before attempting anything else, the culture within the service provider needs to be reviewed to ensure that it will accept and facilitate the implementation of the required changes and improvements. The following key steps need to be completed to achieve this stage of the cycle:

- Establish a **vision**, aligned with the business vision and **objectives**
- Establish the **scope** of the project/**programme**
- Establish a set of high-level objectives
- Establish **governance**, sponsorship and **budget**
- Obtain senior management commitment
- Establish a **culture** focused on:
  - Quality
  - Customer and business focus
  - A learning environment
  - Continual improvement
  - Commitment to the 'improvement cycle'
  - Ownership and accountability.

4.3 DESIGN CONSIDERATIONS IN THE CONTEXT OF AN ORGANIZATION

4.3.1 Where are we now?

Once the **vision** and high-level objectives have been defined, the **service provider** then needs to review the current situation, in terms of what processes are in place and the **maturity** of the organization. The steps and activities that need to be completed here are:

- A **review**, **assessment** or a more formal **audit** of the current situation, using a preferred technique:
  - An internal review or audit
  - Maturity assessment
  - An external assessment or **benchmark**
  - An ISO/IEC 20000 audit
  - An audit against **COBIT**
  - A strengths, weaknesses, opportunities and threats (SWOT) analysis
  - A **risk assessment** and management methodology
- The review should include:
  - The culture and maturity of the **service provider** organization
  - The processes in place and their **capability** and maturity
  - The skills and competence of the people
  - The services and technology
  - The **suppliers**, **contracts** and their capability
  - The **quality** of service and the current measurements, metrics and KPIs
  - A report summarizing the findings and recommendations.

Figure 4.1 – Cultural maturity assessment [15]

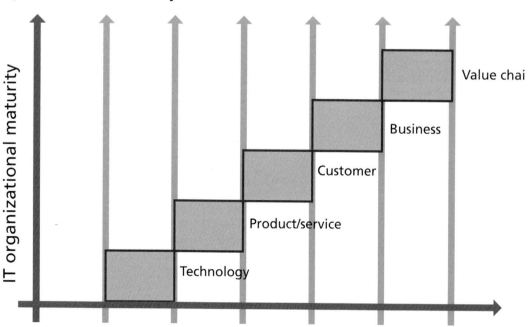

Source Service Design was produced by OGC

Figure 4.2 – Process maturity framework [16]

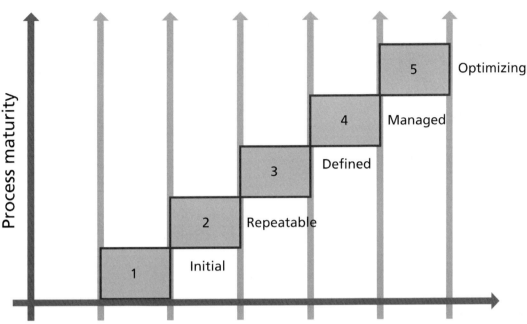

Source Service Design was produced by OGC

The review of the culture should include assessing it in terms of the capability and maturity of the culture within the IT service provider organization, as shown in Figure 4.1.

This assessment should be based on the fact that each growth stage represents a transformation of IT organization and as such will require:

■ Changes in people (skills and competences)

■ Processes and ways of working

■ Technology and tools (to support and enable the people and processes)

■ Steering (the visions, goals and results)

■ Attitude (the values and beliefs)

■ The appropriate level and degree of interaction with the business, stakeholders, customers and users.

The assessment should also include a review of the capability and maturity of the service design processes, as shown in Figure 4.2.

This review and should include all aspects of the processes and their use including the:

■ Vision: steering, objectives and plans

■ Process maturity, functionality, usage, application, effectiveness and efficiency together with ownership, management and documentation

■ People: the roles, responsibilities, skills and knowledge of the people

■ Products, including the tools and technology used to automate the processes

■ Culture: the focus, attitudes and beliefs.

The above framework can be used to provide consistency of process assessment. Assessing these two aspects will determine the current state of the organization and its service management capability and maturity. When starting out on the implementation or improvement of service design, or any set of processes, it is important to build on the strengths of the existing cultures and processes and rapidly identify and improve the weaknesses. A more detailed explanation of this framework is contained in Appendix H of the ITIL v3 Service Design book.

4.4   EXAMPLE SERVICE CATALOGUE

The service catalogue is key document containing valuable information on the complete set of services offered. It should preferably be stored as a set of 'service' CIs within a CMS, maintained under change management. As it is such a valuable set of information it should be available to anyone within the organization. Every new service should immediately be entered into the service catalogue once its initial definition of requirements has been documented and agreed. So as well as the information below, the service catalogue should record the status of every service, through the stages of its defined lifecycle.

Table 4.2 – Example service catalogue [17]

	Service 1	Service2	Service 3	Service …	Service n
Service name					
Service description					
Service type					
Supporting services					
Business owner(s)					
Business unit(s)					
Service manager (s)					
Business impact					
Business priority					
SLA					
Service hours					
Business contacts					
Escalation contacts					
Service reports					
Service reviews					
Security rating					

Source Service Strategy was produced by OGC

SECTION 5 – REPORTING CONSIDERATIONS

SCM:05

The Service Catalogue occupies a unique position within an organization. The Service Catalogue straddles the boundary between the IT service provider and its customers and users. The nature of the Service Catalogue is such that valuable data and information regarding patterns of business activity and demand arise from its usage. This information must be captured and transformed into knowledge to become the basis of wise decisions.

The purpose of reporting is not simply to report operational status, but also to identify, explain and communicate challenges, critical success factors, and risks that impact upon the effectiveness of a Service Catalogue. The transformation of data into information and of information into knowledge and then wisdom is something that should be planned in order to obtain maximum value from a Service Catalogue investment.

The ITIL v3 includes a unique 7-Step Improvement Process that directly applies to the reporting

cycle. Tailoring reporting to specific target groups including senior management, operational management and business can facilitate strategic value beyond simply managing requests for information or providing operational service information.

This section introduces the major challenges and risks facing the creation, development, management and maintenance of a Service Catalogue. It introduces important additional tools including Gantt Charts and Swim Lanes. Finally, it concludes with a discussion of the various Critical Success Factors for a Service Catalogue Management process and solution.

5.1 THE SEVEN-STEP IMPROVEMENT PROCESS

Chapter 3 introduced the seven-step improvement process shown in Figure 5.1. This chapter will go into more detail on this. What do you actually measure and where do you find the information? These are two very important questions and should not be ignored or taken lightly.

Figure 5.1 – Seven-step improvement process [18]

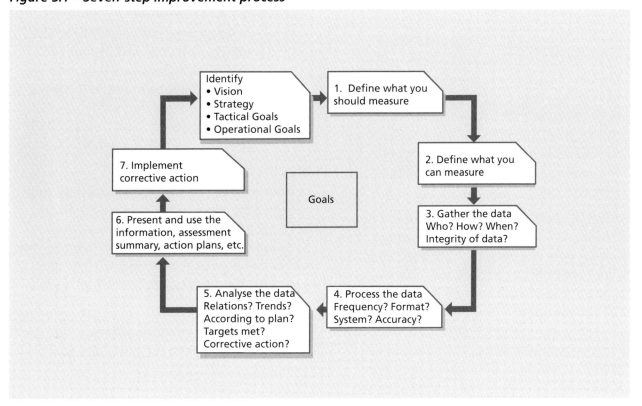

Source Continual Service Improvement was produced by OGC

Steps 1 and 2 are directly related to the **strategic, tactical** and operational goals that have been defined for measuring **services** and service management **processes** as well as the existing technology and **capability** to support measuring and CSI activities.

Steps 1 and 2 are iterative during the rest of the activities. Depending on the goals and **objectives** to support service improvement activities, an organization may have to purchase and install new technology to support the gathering and processing of the data and/or hire staff with the required skills sets.

These two steps are too often ignored because:

■ The process does not include this step. Too often people start gathering information without asking what should be collected in the first place or what they are going to do to with it later. This is common but poor practice.

■ IT knows better. When it comes to data, IT believes, incorrectly, that they know the needs of their customers. The reality is that neither the **customer** nor the IT **organization** sit down together to discuss what should be measured or to identify the purpose of the data in the first place. Even in organizations where SLAs have been signed, they often will include measurement and reporting **requirements** that cannot be met. This always makes for significant customer dissatisfaction issues.

■ Tools are very sophisticated and can gather myriads of data points. IT organizations get lulled into a false sense of security in the knowledge that the data will be there when they need it. Too often the tool is too powerful for the needs of the organization. It is like hammering a small finishing nail using a sledgehammer.

When the data is finally presented (Step 6) without going through the rest of the steps, the results appear incorrect or incomplete. People blame each other, the vendor, the tools, anyone but themselves. Step 1 is crucial. A dialogue must take place between IT and the customer. Goals and objectives must be identified in order to properly identify what should be measured. Based on the goals of the target audience (operational, tactical, or strategic) the service owners need to define what they should measure

in a perfect world. To do this:

■ Map the activities of the service or **service management** processes that need to be measured.

■ Consider what measurements would indicate that each service and service management **activity** is being performed consistently and can determine the health of the process.

Identify the measurements that can be provided based on existing tool sets, organizational **culture** and process **maturity**. Note there may be a gap in what can be measured vs. what should be measured. Quantify the **cost** and business **risk** of this gap to validate any expenditures for tools.

When initially implementing service management processes don't try to measure everything, rather be selective of what measures will help to understand the health of a process. Further chapters will discuss the use of CSFs, KPIs and activity **metrics**. A major mistake many organizations make is trying to do too much in the beginning. Be smart about what you choose to measure.

5.1.1 Step One – Define what you should measure

Question: Where do you actually find the information?

Answer: Talk to the **business**, the customers and to IT management. Utilize the service catalogue as your starting point as well as the **service level requirements** of the different customers. This is the place where you start with the end in mind. In a perfect world, what should you measure? What is important to the business?

Compile a list of what you should measure. This will often be driven by business requirements. Don't try to cover every single eventuality or possible metric in the world. Make it simple. The number of what you should measure can grow quite rapidly. So too can the number of metrics and measurements.

Identify and link the following items:

■ Corporate **vision**, mission, goals and **objectives**

■ IT vision, mission, goals and objectives

■ **Critical success factors**

- Service level targets
- Job description for IT staffs.

Inputs:
- Service level requirements and targets
- Service catalogue
- Vision and mission statements
- Corporate, divisional and departmental goals and objectives
- Legislative requirements
- Governance requirements
- Budget cycle
- Balanced scorecard.

5.1.2 Step Two – Define what you can measure

Every organization may find that they have limitations on what can actually be measured. If you cannot measure something then it should not appear in an SLA.

Question: What do you actually measure?

Answer: Start by listing the tools you currently have in place. These tools will include service management tools, monitoring tools, reporting tools, investigation tools and others. Compile a list of what each tool can currently measure without any configuration or customization. Stay away from customizing the tools as much as possible; configuring them is acceptable

Question: Where do you actually find the information?

Answer: The information is found within each process, procedure and work instruction. The tools are merely a way to collect and provide the data. Look at existing reports and databases. What data is currently being collected and reported on?

Perform a gap analysis between the two lists. Report this information back to the business, the customers and IT management. It is possible that new tools are required or that configuration or customization is required to be able to measure what is required.

Inputs:
- List of what you should measure
- Process flows
- Procedures
- Work instructions
- Technical and user manuals from existing tools
- Existing reports.

5.1.3 Step Three – Gathering the data

Gathering data requires having some form of monitoring in place. Monitoring could be executed using technology such as application, system and component monitoring tools or even be a manual process for certain tasks.

Quality is the key objective of monitoring for continual service improvement. Monitoring will therefore focus on the effectiveness of a service, process, tool, organization or configuration item (CI). The emphasis is not on assuring real-time service performance, rather it is on identifying where improvements can be made to the existing level of service, or IT performance. Monitoring for CSI will therefore tend to focus on detecting exceptions and resolutions. For example, CSI is not as interested in whether an incident was resolved, but whether it was resolved within the agreed time, and whether future incidents can be prevented.

CSI is not only interested in exceptions, though. If a service level agreement is consistently met over time, CSI will also be interested in determining whether that level of performance can be sustained at a lower cost or whether it needs to be upgraded to an even better level of performance. CSI may therefore also need access to regular performance reports.

However since CSI is unlikely to need, or be able to cope with, the vast quantities of data that are produced by all monitoring activity, they will most likely focus on a specific subset of monitoring at any given time. This could be determined by input from the business or improvements to technology.

When a new service is being designed or an existing one changed, this is a perfect opportunity to ensure that what CSI needs to monitor is designed into the service requirements (for further details, see ITIL v3 Service Design book).

This has two main implications:

- **Monitoring** for CSI will change over time. They may be interested in monitoring the e-mail service one quarter, and then move on to look at HR systems in the next quarter.
- This means that **service operation** and CSI need to build a process which will help them to agree on what areas need to be monitored and for what purpose.

It is important to remember that there are three types of **metrics** that an organization will need to collect to support CSI activities as well as other process activities. The types of metrics are:

- Technology metrics – these metrics are often associated with **component** and **application** based metrics such as performance, **availability** etc.
- Process metrics – these metrics are captured in the form of CSFs, KPIs and **activity** metrics for the **service management** processes. These metrics can help determine the overall health of a process. Four key questions that KPIs can help answer are around quality, performance, value and **compliance** of following the process. CSI would use these metrics as input in identifying improvement opportunities for each process.
- Service metrics – these metrics are the results of the end-to-end service. Component/technology metrics are used to compute the service metrics.

Question: What do you actually measure?

Answer: You gather whatever data has been identified as both needed and measurable. Please remember that not all data is gathered automatically. A lot of data is entered manually by people. It is important to ensure that policies are in place to drive the right behaviour to ensure that this manual data entry follows the **SMART** (specific, measurable, achievable, relevant and timely) principle.

As much as possible, you need to standardize the data structure through policies and published **standard**s. For example, how do you enter names in your tools – John Smith; Smith, John or J. Smith? These can be the same or different individuals. Having three different ways of

entering the same name would slow down **trend analysis** and will severely impede any CSI initiative.

Question: Where do you actually find the information?

Answer: IT service management tools, monitoring tools, reporting tools, investigation tools, existing reports and other sources.

Gathering data is defined as the act of monitoring and data collection. This **activity** needs to clearly define the following:

- Who is responsible for monitoring and gathering the data?
- How the data will be gathered?
- When and how often is the data gathered?
- Criteria to evaluate the **integrity** of the data

The answers will be different for every organization.

Service **monitoring** allows weak areas to be identified, so that remedial action can be taken (if there is a justifiable **business case**), thus improving future service quality. Service monitoring also can show where **customer** actions are causing the **fault** and thus lead to identifying where working **efficiency** and/or training can be improved.

Service monitoring should also address both internal and external suppliers since their performance must be evaluated and managed as well.

Service management monitoring helps determine the health and welfare of service management processes in the following manner:

- Process **compliance** – Are the processes being followed? Process compliance seeks to monitor the compliance of the IT **organization** to the new or modified service management processes and also the use of the authorized service management tool that was implemented.
- Quality – How well are the processes working? Monitor the individual or key activities as they relate to the **objective**s of the end-to-end process.
- Performance – How fast or slow? Monitor the process efficiency such as **throughput** or cycle times.

■ Value – Is this making a difference? Monitor the effectiveness and perceived value of the process to the stakeholders and the IT staff executing the process activities.

Monitoring is often associated with automated monitoring of infrastructure components for performance such as availability or capacity, but monitoring should also be used for monitoring staff behaviour such as adherence to process activities, use of authorized tools as well as project schedules and budgets.

Exceptions and alerts need to be considered during the monitoring activity as they can serve as early warning indicators that services are breaking down. Sometimes the exceptions and alerts will come from tools, but they will often come from those who are using the service or service management processes. We don't want to ignore these alerts.

Inputs to gather-the-data activity:
■ New business requirements
■ Existing SLAs
■ Existing monitoring and data capture capability
■ Availability and capacity plans
■ Service improvement plans
■ Previous trend analysis reports
■ List of what you should measure
■ List of what you can measure
■ Gap analysis report
■ List of what to measure
■ Customer satisfaction surveys.

Table 5.1 shows the common procedures to follow in monitoring.

Table 5.1 – Monitoring and data collection procedure [19]

Tasks	Procedures
Task 1	Based on service improvement strategies, goals and objectives plus the business requirements determine what services, systems, applications and/or components as well as service management process activities will require monitoring
	Specify monitoring requirements
	Define data collection requirements, changes in budgets
	Document the outcome
	Get agreement with internal IT
Task 2	Determine frequency of monitoring and data gathering
	Determine method of monitoring and data gathering
Task 3	Define tools required for monitoring and data gathering
	Build, purchase, or modify tools for monitoring and data gathering
	Test the tool
	Install the tool
Task 4	Write monitoring procedures and work instructions when required for monitoring and data collection
Task 5	Produce and communicate monitoring and data collection plan
	Get approval from internal IT and external vendors who may be impacted
Task 6	Update availability and capacity plans if required
Task 7	Begin monitoring and data collection
	Process data into a logical grouping and report format
	Review data to ensure the data make sense

Outputs from gather-the-data activity:
■ Updated availability and capacity plans
■ Monitoring procedures
■ Identified tools to use
■ Monitoring plan
■ Input on IT capability
■ Collection of data
■ Agreement on the integrity of the data.

It is also important in this activity to look at the data that was collected and ask – does this make any sense?

Example
An organization that was developing some management information activities asked a consultant to review the data they had collected. The data was for incident management and the service desk. It was provided in a spreadsheet format and when the consultant opened the spreadsheet it showed that for the month the organization had opened approximately 42,000 new incident tickets and 65,000 incidents tickets

were **closed** on the first contact. It is hard to close more incident tickets than were opened – in other words the data did not make sense.

However, all is not lost. Even if the data did not make any sense, it provides insight into the ability to monitor and gather data, the tools that are used to support monitoring and data gathering and the **procedures** for processing the raw data into a report that can be used for analysis. When investigating the example above, it was discovered that it was a combination on how data was pulled from the tool plus human **error** in inputting the data into a spreadsheet. There was no check and balance before the data was actually processed and presented to key people in the organization.

5.1.4   Step Four – Processing the data

Question: What do you actually do here?

Answer: Convert the data in the required format and for the required audience. Follow the trail from **metric** to KPI to CSF, all the way back to the **vision** if necessary.

Question: Where do you actually find the information?

Answer: IT service management tools, **monitoring** tools, reporting tools, investigation tools, existing reports and other sources.

Once data is gathered, the next step is to process the data into the required format. Report-generating technologies are typically used at this stage as various amounts of data are condensed into information for use in the analysis **activity**. The data is also typically put into a format that provides an end-to-end perspective on the overall **performance** of a **service**. This activity begins the transformation of raw data into packaged information. Use the information to develop insight into the performance of the service and/ or **processes**. Process the data into information (i.e. create logical groupings) which provides a better means to analyse the data – the next activity step in CSI.

The output of logical groupings could be in spreadsheets, reports generated directly from the service management tool suite, **system** monitoring and reporting tools, or telephony tools such as an **automatic call distribution** tool.

Processing the data is an important CSI activity that is often overlooked. While monitoring and collecting data on a single infrastructure **component** is important, it is also important to understand that component's **impact** on the larger infrastructure and **IT service**. Knowing that a **server** was up 99.99% of the time is one thing, knowing that no one could access the server is another. An example of processing the data is taking the data from monitoring of the individual components such as the mainframe, **applications**, WAN, LAN, servers etc and process this into a structure of an end-to-end service from the **customer**'s perspective.

Key questions that need to be addressed in the processing activity are:

- What is the frequency of processing the data? This could be hourly, daily, weekly or monthly. When introducing a new service or **service management** process it is a good idea to monitor and process in shorter intervals than longer intervals. How often analysis and trend investigation activities take place will drive how often the data is processed.

- What format is required for the output? This is also driven by how analysis is done and ultimately how the information is used.

- What tools and systems can be used for processing the data?

- How do we evaluate the accuracy of the processed data?

There are two aspects to data gathering. One is automated and the other is manual. While both are important and contribute greatly to the measuring process, accuracy is a major differentiator between the two types. The accuracy of the automated data gathering and processing is not the issue here. The vast majority of CSI-related data will be gathered by automated means. Human data gathering and processing is the issue. It is important for staff to properly document their **compliance** activities, to update logs and **records**. Common excuses are that people are too busy, that this is not important or that it is not their job. On-going communication about the benefits of performing administrative tasks is of utmost importance. Tying these administrative tasks to job performance is one way to alleviate this issue.

Inputs to processing-the-data **activity**:

■ Data collected through **monitoring**

■ Reporting **requirements**

■ SLAs

■ OLAs

■ **Service catalogue**

■ List of **metrics**, KPI, CSF, **objectives** and goals

■ Report frequency

■ Report template.

Table 5.2 shows common **procedures** for processing data activity

A flow diagram is nice to look at and it gracefully summarizes the procedure but it does not contain all the required information. It is important to translate the flow diagram into a more meaningful way for people to understand the procedure with the appropriate level of detail including **roles** and responsibilities, timeframes, input and outputs, and more.

Table 5.2 – Procedure for processing data activity [20]

Tasks	Procedures
Task 1	Based on **strategy**, goals and SLAs, define the data processing requirements
Task 2	Determine frequency of processing the data Determine method of processing the data
Task 3	Identify and document the format of logical grouping of data elements Define tools required for processing data Build, purchase or modify tools for measuring Test tool Install tool
Task 4	Develop processing data procedures Train people on procedures
Task 5	Develop and communicate monitoring plan Get approval from internal IT and external vendors who may be impacted
Task 6	Update availability and capacity plans if required
Task 7	Begin the data processing
Task 8	Process into logical groupings
Task 9	Evaluate processed data for accuracy

Outputs of processing-the-data activity:

While it is important to identify the outputs of each **activity** such as data and decisions it is even more important to determine the output of the **procedure**, the level of detail, the quality, the format etc.

Examples of outputs from procedures:

■ Updated **availability** and capacity plans

■ Reports

■ Logical groupings of data ready for analysis.

5.1.5   Step Five – Analysing the data

Your organization's **service desk** has a trend of reduced **call** volumes consistently over the last four months. Even though this is a trend, you need to ask yourself the question: 'Is this a good trend or a bad trend?' You don't know if the call reduction is because you have reduced the number of recurring errors in the infrastructure by good **problem management** activities or if the **customers** feel that the service desk doesn't provide any value and they have started bypassing the service desk and going directly to second-level **support groups**.

Data analysis transforms the information into knowledge of the **events** that are affecting the **organization**. More skill and experience is required to perform data analysis than data gathering and processing. **Verification** against goals and objectives is expected during this activity. This verification validates that objectives are being supported and value is being added. It is not sufficient to simply produce graphs of various types but to document the observations and conclusions.

Question: What do you actually analyse?

Answer: Once the data is processed into information, you can then analyse the results, looking for answers to questions such as:

■ Are there any clear trends?

■ Are they positive or negative trends?

■ Are changes required?

■ Are we operating according to plan?

■ Are we meeting targets?

■ Are corrective actions required?

■ Are there underlying structural **problems**?

■ What is the **cost** of the service gap?

Question: Where do you actually find the information?

Answer: Here you apply knowledge to your information. Without this, you have nothing more than sets of numbers showing metrics that are meaningless. It is not enough to simply look at this month's figures and accept them without question, even if they meet SLA targets. You should analyse the figures to stay ahead of the game. Without analysis you merely have information. With analysis you have knowledge. If you find anomalies or poor results, then look for ways to improve.

It is interesting to note the number of job titles for IT professionals that contain the word 'analyst' and even more surprising to discover that few of them actually analyse anything. This step takes time. It requires concentration, knowledge, skills, experience etc. One of the major assumptions is that the automated processing, reporting, monitoring tool has actually done the analysis. Too often people simply point at a trend and say 'Look, numbers have gone up over the last quarter.' However, key questions need to be asked, such as:

- Is this good?
- Is this bad?
- Is this expected?
- Is this in line with targets?

Combining multiple data points on a graph may look nice but the real question is what does it actually mean. 'A picture is worth a thousand words' goes the saying. In analysing the data an accurate question would be 'Which thousand words?' To transform this data into knowledge, compare the information from step 3 against both the requirements from step 1 and what could realistically be measured from step 2.

Be sure to also compare against the clearly defined objectives with measurable targets that were set in the service design, transition and operations lifecycle stages. Confirmation needs to be sought that these objectives and the milestones were reached. If not, have improvement initiatives been implemented? If so, then the CSI activities start again from the gathering data, processing

data and analysing data to identify if the desired improvement in service quality has been achieved. At the completion of each significant stage or milestone, a review should be conducted to ensure the objectives have been met. It is possible here to use the post-implementation review (PIR) from the change management process. The PIR will include a review of supporting documentation and the general awareness amongst staff of the refined processes or service. A comparison is required of what has been achieved against the original goals.

During the analysis activity, but after the results are compiled and analysis and trend evaluation have occurred, it is recommended that internal meetings be held within IT to review the results and collectively identify improvement opportunities. It is important to have these internal meetings before you begin presenting and using the information which is the next activity of continual service improvement. The result is that IT is a key player in determining how the results and any actions items are presented to the business.

This puts IT in a better position to formulate a plan of presenting the results and any action items to the business and to senior IT management. Throughout this publication the terms 'service' and 'service management' have been used extensively. IT is too often focused on managing the various systems used by the business, often (but incorrectly) equating service and system. A service is actually made up of systems. Therefore if IT wants to be perceived as a key player, then IT must move from a systems-based organization to a service-based organization. This transition will force the improvement of communication between the different IT silos that exist in many IT organizations.

Performing proper analysis on the data also places the business in a position to make strategic, tactical and operational decisions about whether there is a need for service improvement. Unfortunately, the analysis activity is often not done. Whether it is due to a lack of resources with the right skills and/or simply a lack of time is unclear. What is clear is that without proper analysis, errors will continue to occur and mistakes will continue to be repeated. There will be little improvement.

Data analysis transforms the information into knowledge of the events that are affecting the organization. As an example, a sub-activity of capacity management is workload management. This can be viewed as analysing the data to determine which customers use what resource, how they use the resource, when they use the resource and how this impacts the overall performance of the resource. You will also be able to see if there is a trend on the usage of the resource over a period of time. From an incremental improvement process this could lead to some focus on demand management, or influencing the behaviour of customers.

Consideration must be given to the skills required to analyse from both a technical viewpoint and from an interpretation viewpoint.

When analysing data, it is important to seek answers to questions such as:

- Are operations running according to plan? This could be a project plan, financial plan, availability, capacity or even IT service continuity management plan.

- Are targets defined in SLAs or the service catalogue being met?

- Are there underlying structural problems that can be identified?

- Are corrective actions required?

- Are there any trends? If so then what are the trends showing? Are they positive trends or negative trends?

- What is leading to or causing the trends?

Reviewing trends over a period of time is another important task. It is not good enough to see a 'snapshot' of a data point at a specific moment in time, but to look at the data points over a period of time. How did we do this month compared to last month, this quarter compared to last quarter, this year compared to last year?

It is not enough to only look at the results but also to look at what led to the results for the current period. If we had a bad month, did we have an anomaly that took place? Is this a demonstrable trend or simply a one-off?

Example
When one organization started performing trend

analysis activities around incident management, they discovered that their number of incidents increased for a one month period every three months. When they investigated the cause, they found it was tied directly to a quarterly release of an application change. This provided statistical data for them to review the effectiveness of their change and release management processes as well as understand the impact each release would have on the service desk with the number of increased call volumes. The service desk was also able to begin identifying key skill sets needed to support this specific application.

Trends are an indicator that more analysis is needed to understand what is causing it. When a trend goes up or down it is a signal that further investigation is needed to determine if it is positive or negative.

Another example
A change manager communicates that the change management process is doing well because the volume of requests for changes has steadily decreased. Is this positive or negative? If problem management is working well, it could be positive as recurring incidents are removed therefore fewer changes are required as the infrastructure is more stable. However, if users have stopped submitting requests for changes because the process is not meeting expectations, the trend is negative.

Without analysis the data is merely information. With analysis comes improvement opportunities.

Throughout CSI, assessment should identify whether targets were achieved and, if so, whether new targets (and therefore new KPIs) need to be defined. If targets were achieved but the perception has not improved, then new targets may need to be set and new measures put in place to ensure that these new targets are being met.

When analysing the results from process metrics keep in mind that a process will only be as efficient as its limited bottleneck activity. So if the analysis shows that a process activity is not efficient and continually creates a bottleneck then this would be a logical place to begin looking for a process improvement opportunity.

5.1.6 Step Six – Presenting and using the information

The sixth step is to take our knowledge and present it, that is, turn it into wisdom by utilizing reports, monitors, action plans, reviews, evaluations and opportunities. Consider the target audience; make sure that you identify exceptions to the service, benefits that have been revealed, or can be expected. Data gathering occurs at the operational level of an organization. Format this data into knowledge that all levels can appreciate and gain insight into their needs and expectations.

Question: What do you actually measure?

Answer: There are no measurements in this step.

Question: Where do you actually find the information?

Answer: From all previous steps.

5.1.6.1 Historical/previous presentations

This stage involves presenting the information in a format that is understandable, at the right level, provides value, notes exceptions to service, identifies benefits that were revealed during the time period, and allows those receiving the information to make strategic, tactical and operational decisions. In other words, presenting the information in the manner that makes it the most useful for the target audience.

Creating reports and presenting information is an activity that is done in most organizations to some extent or another; however it often is not done well. For many organizations this activity is simply taking the gathered raw data (often straight from the tool) and reporting this same data to everyone. There has been no processing and analysis of the data.

The other issue often associated with presenting and using information it that it is overdone. Managers at all levels are bombarded with too many e-mails, too many meetings, too many reports. Too often they are copied and presented to as part of an I-am-covering-my-you-know-what exercise. The reality is that the managers often don't need this information or at the very least, not in that format. There often is a lack of what role the manager has in making decisions and providing guidance on improvement programmes.

As we have discussed, continual service improvement is an ongoing activity of monitoring and gathering data, processing the data into logical groupings, analysing the data for meeting targets, identifying trends and identifying improvement opportunities. There is no value in all the work done to this point if we don't do a good job of presenting our findings and then using those findings to make improvement decisions.

Begin with the end in mind is habit number 2 in Stephen Covey's publication *Seven Habits of Highly Effective People* (Simon & Schuster, 1989). Even though the publication is about personal leadership, the habit holds true with presenting and using information. In addition to understanding the target audience, it is also important to understand the report's purpose. If the purpose and value cannot be articulated, then it is important to question if it is needed at all.

There are usually three distinct audiences:

- **The business** – Their real need is to understand whether IT delivered the service they promised at the levels they promised and if not, what corrective actions are being implemented to improve the situation.
- **Senior (IT) management** – This group is often focused on the results surrounding CSFs and KPIs such as, customer satisfaction, actual vs. plan, costing and revenue targets. Information provided at this level helps determine strategic and tactical improvements on a larger scale. Senior (IT) management often wants this type of information provided in the form of a balanced scorecard or IT scorecard format to see the big picture at one glance.
- **Internal IT** – This group is often interested in KPIs and activity metrics that help them plan, coordinate, schedule and identify incremental improvement opportunities.

Often there is a gap between what IT reports and what is of interest to the business. IT is famous for reporting availability in percentages such as 99.85% available. In most cases this is not calculated from an end-to-end perspective but only mainframe availability or application availability and often doesn't take into consideration LAN/WAN, server or desktop downtime. In reality, most people in IT don't know the difference between 99.95% and 99.99% availability let alone the business. Yet reports continue to show availability achievements in percentages. What the business really wants to understand is the number of outages that occurred and the duration of the outages with analysis describing the impact on the business processes, in essence, unavailability expressed in a commonly understood measure – time.

Now more than ever, IT must invest the time to understand specific business goals and translate IT metrics to reflect an impact against these goals. Businesses invest in tools and services that affect productivity, and support should be one of those services. The major challenge, and one that can be met, is to effectively communicate the business benefits of a well-run IT support group. The starting point is a new perspective on goals, measures, and reporting, and how IT actions affect business results. You will then be prepared to answer the question: 'How does IT help to generate value for your company?'

Although most reports tend to concentrate on areas where things are not going as well as hoped for, do not forget to report on the good news as well. A report showing improvement trends is IT services' best marketing vehicle. It is vitally important that reports show whether CSI has

actually improved the overall service provision and if it has not, the actions taken to rectify the situation.

The figure below is an example of a SLA monitoring chart that provides a visual representation of an organization's ability to meet defined targets over a period of months.

Some of the common problems associated with the presenting and reporting activity:

■ Everyone gets the same report (business, senior management and IT managers).

■ The format is not what people want. It is important to understand the audience and how they like to receive information. Some like the information in text format, some in graphs, pie charts etc. It is hard to please everyone, but getting agreement on the report format is a step in the right direction.

This is why many organizations are moving to a balanced scorecard or IT scorecard concept. This concept can start at the business level, then the IT level, and then functional groups and/or services within IT.

■ Lack of an executive summary – the executive summary should discuss the current results, what led to the results and what actions have or will be taken to address any issues.

Figure 5.2 – Service level achievement chart [21]

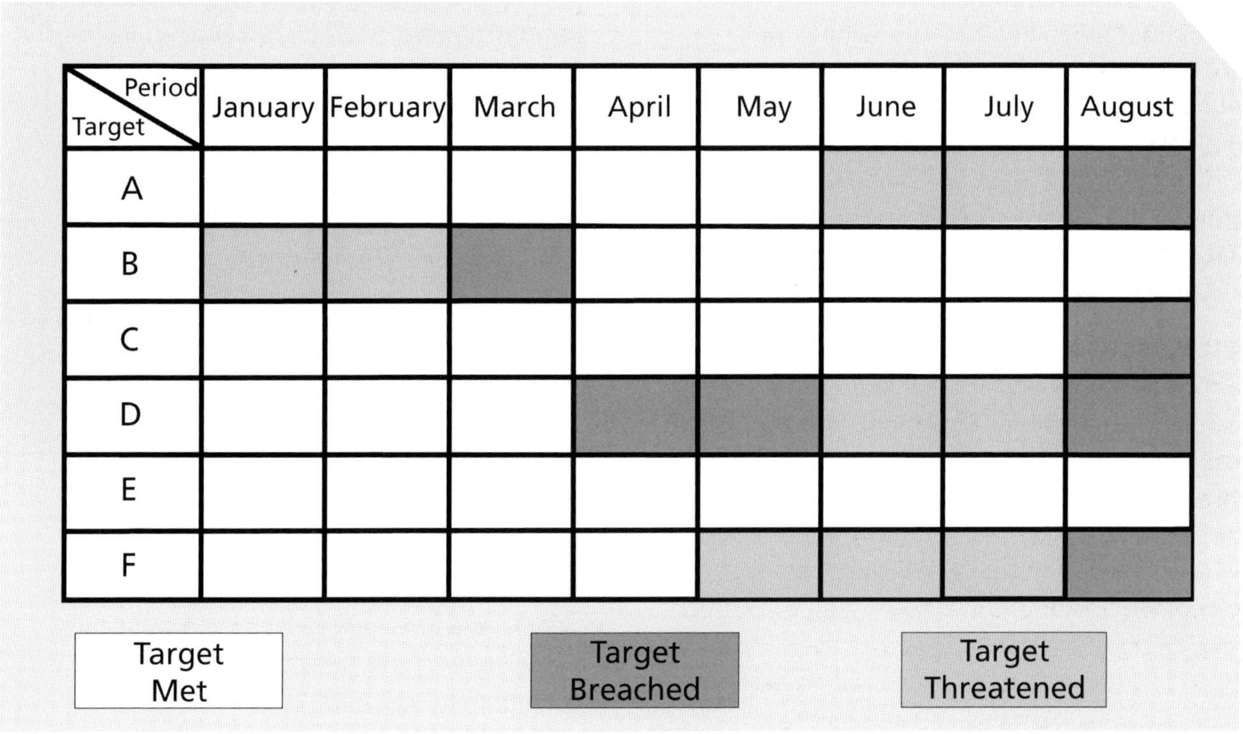

Period / Target	January	February	March	April	May	June	July	August
A						(threatened)	(threatened)	(breached)
B	(threatened)	(threatened)	(breached)					
C								(breached)
D				(breached)	(breached)	(threatened)	(threatened)	(breached)
E								
F					(threatened)	(threatened)		(breached)

Target Met	Target Breached	Target Threatened

Source Continual Service Improvement was produced by OGC

- Reports are not linked to any baseline, IT scorecard or balanced scorecard.

- Too much supporting data provided.

- Reports are presented in terms that are not understandable. For example, availability is reported in percentages when the business often is interested in knowing the number, duration and impact of outages.

The resources required to produce, verify and distribute reports should not be under-estimated. Even with automation, this can be a time-consuming activity.

5.1.7 Step Seven – Implementing corrective action

Use the knowledge gained to optimize, improve and correct services. Managers need to identify issues and present solutions. Explain how the corrective actions to be taken will improve the service.

Example

An organization hired an expensive consulting firm to assess the maturity of the processes against the ITIL framework. The report from the consulting organization had the following observation and recommendation about the incident management process:

The help desk is not doing incident management the way ITIL does. Our recommendation is that you must implement incident management.

The reaction from the customer was simple. They fired the consulting organization.

What would happen to you if you presented a similar observation and recommendation to your CIO?

CSI identifies many opportunities for improvement however organizations cannot afford to implement all of them. Based on goals, objectives and types of service breaches, an organization needs to prioritize improvement activities. Improvement initiatives can also be externally driven by regulatory requirements, changes in competition, or even political decisions.

If organizations were implementing corrective action according to CSI, there would be no

need for this publication. Corrective action is often done in reaction to a single event that caused a (severe) outage to part or all of the organization. Other times, the squeaky wheel will get noticed and specific corrective action will be implemented in no relation to the priorities of the organization, thus taking valuable resources away from real emergencies. This is common practice but obviously not best practice.

After a decision to improve a service and/ or service management process is made, then the service lifecycle continues. A new service strategy may be defined, service design builds the changes, service transition implements the changes into production and then service operation manages the day-to-day operations of the service and/or service management processes. Keep in mind that CSI activities continue through each phase of the service lifecycle.

Each service lifecycle phase requires resources to build or modify the services and/or service management processes, potential new technology or modifications to existing technology, potential changes to KPIs and other metrics and possibly even new or modified OLAs/UCs to support SLAs. Communication, training and documentation is required to transition a new/improved service, tool or service management process into production.

Example of corrective action being implemented

A financial organization with a strategically important website continually failed to meet its operational targets, especially with regard to the quality of service delivered by the site. The prime reason for this was their lack of focus on the monitoring of operational events, service availability and response. This situation was allowed to develop until senior business managers demanded action from the senior IT management. There were major repercussions, and reviews were undertaken to determine the underlying cause. After considerable pain and disruption, an operations group was identified to monitor this particular service. A part of the requirement was the establishment of weekly internal reviews and weekly reports on operational performance. Operational events were immediately investigated whenever they occurred and were individually reviewed after resolution. An improvement team was established, with representation from all areas, to implement the recommendations from the reviews and the feedback from the monitoring group. This eventually resulted in considerable improvement in the quality of service delivered to the business and its customers.

Often steps are forgotten or are taken for granted or someone assumes that someone else has completed the step. This indicates a breakdown in the process and a lack of understanding of roles and responsibilities. The harsh reality is that some steps are overdone while others are incomplete or overlooked.

There are various levels or orders of management in an organization. Individuals need to know where to focus their activities. Line managers need to show overall performance and improvement. Directors need to show that quality and performance targets are being met, while risk is being minimized. Overall, senior management need to know what is going on so that they can make informed choices and exercise judgement. Each order has its own perspective. Understanding these perspectives is where maximum value of information is leveraged.

Understanding the order your intended audience occupies and their drivers helps you present the issues and benefits of your process. At the highest level of the organization are the strategic thinkers. Reports need to be short, quick to read and aligned to their drivers. Discussions about risk avoidance, protecting the image or brand of the organization, profitability and cost savings are compelling reasons to support your improvement efforts.

The second order consists of vice presidents and directors. Reports can be more detailed, but need to summarize findings over time. Identifying how processes support the business objectives, early warning around issues that place the business at risk, and alignment to existing measurement frameworks that they use are strong methods you can use to sell the process benefits to them.

The third order consists of managers and high level supervisors. Compliance to stated objectives, overall team and process performance, insight into resource constraints and continual

improvement initiatives are their drivers. Measurements and reports need to market how these are being supported by the process outputs.

Lastly at the fourth level of the hierarchy are the staff members and team leaders. At a personal level, the personal benefits need to be emphasized. Therefore metrics that show their individual performance, provide recognition of their skills (and gaps in skills) and identify training opportunities are essential in getting these people to participate in the processes willingly.

CSI is often viewed as an ad hoc activity within IT services. The activity usually kicks in when someone in IT management yells loud enough. This is not the right way to address CSI. Often these reactionary events are not even providing continual improvement, but simply stopping a single failure from occurring again.

CSI takes a commitment from everyone in IT working throughout the service lifecycle to be successful at improving services and service management processes. It requires ongoing attention, a well-thought-out plan, consistent attention to monitoring, analysing and reporting results with an eye toward improvement. Improvements can be incremental in nature but also require a huge commitment to implement a new service or meet new business requirements.

This section spelled out the seven steps of CSI activities. All seven steps need attention. There is no reward for taking a short cut or not addressing each step in a sequential nature. If any step is missed, there is a risk of not being efficient and effective in meeting the goals of CSI.

IT services must ensure that proper staffing and tools are identified and implemented to support CSI activities. It is also important to understand the difference between what should be measured and what can be measured. Start small – don't expect to measure everything at once. Understand the organizational capability to gather data and process the data. Be sure to spend time analysing data as this is where the real value comes in. Without analysis of the data, there is no real opportunity to truly improve services or service management processes. Think through the strategy and plan for reporting and using the data. Reporting is partly a marketing activity. It is important that IT focus on the value added to the organization as well as reporting on issues and achievements. In order for steps 5 to 7 to be carried out correctly, it is imperative that the target audience is considered when packaging the information.

An organization can find improvement opportunities throughout the entire service lifecycle. An IT organization does not need to wait until a service or service management process is transitioned into the operations area to begin identifying improvement opportunities.

5.1.8 Integration with the rest of the lifecycle stages and service management processes

In order to support improvement activities it is important to have CSI integrated within each lifecycle stage including the underlying processes residing in each lifecycle phase.

5.1.9 Monitoring and data collection throughout the service lifecycle

Service strategy is responsible for monitoring the progress of strategies, standards, policies and architectural decisions that have been made and implemented.

Service design monitors and gathers data associated with creating and modifying (design efforts) of services and service management processes. This part of the service lifecycle also measures against the effectiveness and ability to measure CSFs and KPIs that were defined through gathering business requirements. Service design also defines what should be measured. This would include monitoring project schedules, progress to project milestones, and project results against goals and objectives.

Service transition develops the monitoring procedures and criteria to be used during and after implementation. Service transition monitors and gathers data on the actual release into production of services and service management processes. It is the responsibility of service transition to ensure that the services and service management processes are embedded in a way that can be managed and maintained according to the strategies and design efforts. Service transition develops the monitoring procedures and criteria to be used during and after implementation. Service operation is responsible for the actual monitoring of services in the production environment. Service operation plays a large part in the processing activity. Service operation provides input into what can be measured and processed into logical groupings as well as doing the actual processing of the data. Service operation would also be responsible for taking the component data and processing it in the format to provide a better end-to-end perspective of the service achievements.

CSI receives the collected data as input in the remainder of CSI activities.

5.1.10 Role of other processes in monitoring and data collection

5.1.10.1 Service level management

SLM plays a key role in the data gathering activity as SLM is responsible for not only defining business requirements but also IT's capabilities to achieve them.

- One of the first items in defining IT's capabilities is to identify what monitoring and data collection activities are currently taking place

- SLM then needs to look at what is happening with the monitoring data. Is the monitoring taking place only at a component level and, if so, is anyone looking at multiple components to provide an end-to-end service performance perspective?

- SLM should also identify who gets the data, whether any analysis takes place on the data before it is presented, and if any trend evaluation is undertaken to understand the performance over a period of time. This information will be helpful in following CSI activities

- Through the negotiation process with the business, SLM would define what to measure and which aspects to report. This would in turn drive the monitoring and data collection requirements. If there is no capability to monitor and/or collect data on an item then it should not appear in the SLA. SLM should be a part of the review process to monitor results

- SLM is responsible for developing and getting agreement on OLAs and UCs that require internal or external monitoring.

5.1.10.2 Availability and capacity management

■ Provide significant input into existing monitoring and data collection capabilities, tool requirements to meet new data collection requirements and ensuring the availability and capacity plans are updated to reflect new or modified monitoring and data collection requirements

■ Are accountable for the actual infrastructure monitoring and data collection activities that take place. Therefore roles and responsibilities need to be defined and the roles filled with properly skilled and trained staff

■ Are accountable for ensuring tools are in place to gather data

■ Are accountable for ensuring that the actual monitoring and data collection activities are consistently performed.

5.1.10.3 Incident management and service desk

■ Incident management can define monitoring requirements to support event and incident detection through automation and also has the ability to automatically open incident tickets and/or auto-escalate incident tickets

■ Event and incident monitoring can identify abnormal situations and conditions which helps with predicting and pre-empting situations and conditions thereby avoiding possible service and component failures

■ Monitoring the response times, repair times, resolution times and incident escalations

■ As a single point of contact it is important for the service desk to monitor telephony items such as call volumes, average speed of answer, call abandonment rates etc. so that immediate action can be taken when there is an increase in contacts to the service desk. This would also apply to those service desks who provide support via e-mail and via the web.

5.1.10.4 Security management
Security management contributes to monitoring and data collection in the following manner:

■ Define security monitoring and data collection requirements

■ Monitor, verify and track the levels of security according to the organizational security policies and guidelines

■ Assist in determining effects of security measures on the data monitoring and collection from the confidentiality (accessible only to those who should), integrity (data is accurate and not corrupted or not corruptible) and availability (data is available when needed) perspectives.

5.1.10.5 Financial management
Financial management is responsible for monitoring and collecting data associated with the actual expenditures vs. budget and is able to provide input on questions such as: are costing or revenue targets on track? Financial management should also monitor the ongoing cost per service etc.

In addition financial management will provide the necessary templates to assist CSI to create the budget and expenditure reports for the various improvement initiatives as well as providing the means to compute the ROI of the improvements.

5.1.11 Role of other processes in measuring the data

5.1.11.1 Service level management
SLM supports the CSI processing data activity in the following manner:

■ Define requirements to support any default levels of service that are described in the service catalogue

■ Ensure that the SLAs only incorporate measurements that truly can be measured and reported on

■ Negotiate and document OLAs and UCs that define the required measurements

■ Review the results of the processed data from an end-to-end approach

■ Help define the reporting frequency of processing and reporting formats.

5.1.11.2 Availability and capacity management

■ Availability and capacity management would be responsible for processing the data at a component level and then working with SLM providing the data in an end-to-end perspective

■ Process data on KPIs such as availability or performance measures

■ Utilize the agreed upon reporting formats

■ Analyse processed data for accuracy.

5.1.11.3 Incident management and service desk

■ Process data on **incidents** and **service requests** such as who is using the service desk and what is the nature of the incidents

■ Collect and processing data on KPIs such as mean time to restore service and percentage of incidents resolved within service targets

■ Process data for telephony statistics such as number of inbound/outbound calls, average talk time, average speed of answer, abandoned calls etc.

■ Utilize the agreed upon reporting format

■ Analyse processed data for accuracy.

5.1.11.4 Security management

■ Process response and **resolution** data on **security** incidents

■ Create trend analyses on security breaches

■ Validate success of **risk** mitigation strategies

■ Utilize the agreed upon reporting format

■ Analyse processed data for accuracy.

5.1.12 Analysing the data throughout the service lifecycle

Service strategy analyses results associated with implemented strategies, policies and **standards**. This would include identifying any trends, comparing results against goals and also identifying any improvement opportunities.

Service design analyses current results of **design** and **project** activities. Trends are also noted with results compared against the design goals. Service design also identifies improvement opportunities and analyses the **effectiveness** and ability to measure CSFs and KPIs that were defined when gathering business requirements.

Service operation analyses current results as well as trends over a period of time. Service operation also identifies both incremental and large-scale improvement opportunities, providing input into what can be measured and processed into logical groupings. This area also performs the actual data processing. Service operation would also be responsible for taking the **component** data and processing it in the format to provide a better end-to-end perspective of **service** achievements. If there is a CSI functional group within an **organization**, this group can be the single

point for combining all analysis, trend data and comparison of results to targets. This group could then review all proposed improvement opportunities and help prioritize the opportunities and finally make a consolidated recommendation to senior management. For smaller organizations, this may fall to an individual or smaller group acting as a coordinating point and owning CSI. This is a key point. Too often data is gathered in the various technical domains … never to be heard from again. Designating a CSI group provides a single place in the organization for all the data to reside and be analysed.

5.1.13 Role of other processes in analysing the data

5.1.13.1 Service level management
SLM supports the CSI **process** data **activity** in the following manner:

■ Analyse the service level achievements compared to SLAs and **service level targets** that may be associated with the service catalogue

■ Document and review trends over a period of time to identify any consistent patterns

■ Identify the need for service improvement **plans**

■ Identify the need to modify existing OLAs or UCs.

5.1.13.2 Availability and capacity management

■ Analyse and identify trends on component and service data

■ Compare results with prior months, quarters or annual reports

■ Identify the need for updating the need for improvement in gathering and processing data

■ Analyse the **performance** of components against defined technical **specifications**

■ Document and review trends over a period of time to identify any consistent patterns

■ Identify the need for service improvement **plans** or corrective actions

■ Analyse processed data for accuracy.

5.1.13.3 Incident management and service desk

■ Document and review **incident** trends on incidents, service requests and telephony statistics over a period of time to identify any consistent patterns

- Compare results with prior months, quarters or annual reports
- Compare results with agreed-to levels of service
- Identify the need for service improvement plans or corrective actions
- Analyse processed data for accuracy.

5.1.13.4 Problem management

Problem management plays a key role in the analysis activity as this process supports all the other processes with regards to trend identification and performing root cause analysis. Problem management is usually associated with reducing incidents, but a good problem management process is also involved in helping define process-related problems as well as those associated with services.

Overall, problem management seeks to:

- Perform root cause investigation as to what is leading identified trends
- Recommend improvement opportunities
- Compare results with prior results
- Compare results to agreed to service levels.

5.1.13.5 Security management

Security management as a function relies on the activities of all other processes to help determine the cause of security related incidents and problems. The security management function will submit requests for changes to implement corrections or for new updates to, say, the anti-virus software. Other processes such as availability (confidentiality, integrity, availability and recoverability), capacity (capacity and performance) and service continuity management (planning on how to handle crisis) will lend a hand in planning longer term. In turn security management will play a key role in assisting CSI regarding all security aspects of improvement initiatives or for security-related improvements.

- Document and review security incidents for the current time period
- Compare results with prior results
- Identify the need for SIP or corrective actions
- Analyse processed data for accuracy.

5.1.14 Presenting and using the information throughout the service lifecycle

Service strategy presents current results, trends and recommendations for improvement associated with implemented strategies, policies and standards.

Service design presents current results, trends and recommendations for improvement of design and project activities.

Service transition presents current results, trends and recommendations for moving services and service management processes into production.

Service operation presents current results, trends and recommendations on improvement initiatives for both services and service management processes.

5.1.15 Role of other processes in presenting and using the information

5.1.15.1 Service level management

SLM presents information to the business and discusses the service achievements for the current time period as well as any longer trends that were identified. These discussions should also include information about what led to the results and any incremental or fine-tuning actions required. Overall, SLM:

- Conducts consistent service review meetings (internal and external)
- Supports the preparation of reports
- Updates the SLA monitoring chart (SLAM) (see ITIL v3 Service Design book, Chapter 9 for further details on the SLAM chart)
- Provides input into prioritizing improvement activities.

5.1.15.2 Availability and capacity management

- Supports preparation of the reports
- Provides input into prioritizing SIP or corrective actions
- Implements incremental or fine-tuning activities that do not require business approval.

5.1.15.3 Incident management and service desk

- Supports preparation of the reports
- Provides input into prioritizing SIPs or

corrective actions

- Implements incremental or fine-tuning activities that do not require business approval.

5.1.15.4 Problem management

- Provides input into service improvement initiatives and prioritizes improvement initiatives
- Security management
- Supports preparation of the reports
- Provides input into prioritizing SIP or corrective actions
- Implements incremental or fine-tuning activities that do not require business approval.

5.1.16 Role of other processes in implementing corrective action

5.1.16.1 Change management

When CSI determines that an improvement to a service is warranted, an RFC must be submitted to change management. In turn change management treats the RFC like any other RFC. The RFC is prioritized and categorized according to policies and procedures defined in the change management process. Release and deployment management, as a part of service transition, is responsible for moving this change to the production environment. Once the change is implemented, CSI is part of the PIR to assess the success or failure of the change.

Representatives from CSI should be part of the CAB and the CAB/EC. Changes have an effect on service provision and may also affect other CSI initiatives. As part of the CAB and CAB/EC, CSI is in a better position to provide feedback and react to upcoming changes.

5.1.16.2 Service level management

The SLM process often generates a good starting point for a service improvement plan (SIP) – and the service review process may drive this. Where an underlying difficulty that is adversely impacting service quality is identified, SLM must, in conjunction with problem management and availability management, instigate a SIP to identify and implement whatever actions are necessary to overcome the difficulties and restore service quality. SIP initiatives may also focus on such issues as training, system testing and documentation. In these cases, the relevant people need to be involved and adequate

feedback given to make improvements for the future. At any time, a number of separate initiatives that form part of the SIP may be running in parallel to address difficulties with a number of services.

Some organizations have established an up-front annual budget held by SLM from which SIP initiatives can be funded.

If an organization is outsourcing delivery of service to a third party, the issue of service improvement should be discussed at the outset and covered (and budgeted for) in the contract, otherwise there is no incentive during the lifetime of the contract for the supplier to improve service targets.

There may be incremental improvement or large-scale improvement activities within each stage of the service lifecycle. As already mentioned, one of the activities IT management have to address is prioritization of service improvement opportunities.

5.2   METRICS AND MEASUREMENT

It is important to remember that there are three types of metrics that an organization will need to collect to support CSI activities as well as other process activities. The types of metrics are:

- **Technology metrics** – These metrics are often associated with component and application-based metrics such as performance, availability etc.
- **Process metrics** – These metrics are captured in the form of CSFs, KPIs and activity metrics for the service management processes. These metrics can help determine the overall health of a process. Four key questions that KPIs can help answer are around quality, performance, value and compliance of following the process. CSI would use these metrics as input in identifying improvement opportunities for each process.
- **Service metrics** – These metrics are the results of the end-to-end service. Component metrics are used to compute the service metrics.

In general, a metric is a scale of measurement defined in terms of a standard, i.e. in terms of a well-defined unit. The quantification of an event through the process of measurement relies on the existence of an explicit or implicit metric, which is the standard to which measurements are referenced.

Metrics are a system of parameters or ways of quantitative **assessment** of a process that is to be measured, along with the processes to carry out such measurement. Metrics define what is to be measured. Metrics are usually specialized by the subject area, in which case they are valid only within a certain domain and cannot be directly benchmarked or interpreted outside it. Generic metrics, however, can be aggregated across subject areas or business **units** of an enterprise.

Metrics are used in several business **models** including CMMI They are used in **knowledge management** (KM). These measurements or metrics can be used to track trends, productivity, resources and much more. Typically, the metrics tracked are KPIs.

5.2.1 How many CSFs and KPIs?

The opinions on this are varied. Some recommended that no more than two to three KPIs are defined per CSF at any given time and that a service or process has no more that two to three CSFs associated with it at any given time

while others recommend upwards of four to five. This may not sound much but when considering the number of services, processes or when using the **balanced scorecard** approach, the upper limit can be staggering!

It is recommended that in the early stages of a CSI **programme** only two to three KPIs for each CSF are defined, monitored and reported on. As the **maturity** of a service and service management processes increase, additional KPIs can be added. Based on what is important to the business and IT management the KPIs may change over a period of time. Also keep in mind that as service management processes are implemented this will often change the KPIs of other processes. As an example, increasing first-contact **resolution** is a common KPI for **incident management**. This is a good KPI to begin with, but when you implement **problem management** this should change. One of problem management's **objectives** is to reduce the number of recurring **incidents**. When these types of recurring incidents are reduced this will reduce the number of first-contact resolutions. In this case a reduction in first-contact resolution is a positive trend.

Figure 5.3 – From CSF to measurement [22]

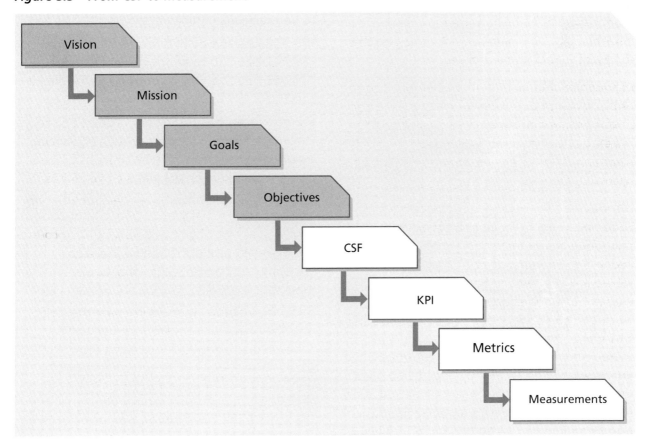

Source Continual Service Improvement was produced by OGC

The next step is to identify the metrics and measurements required to compute the KPI. There are two basic kinds of KPI, qualitative and quantitative.

Here is a qualitative example:
CSF: Improving IT service quality
KPI: 10 percent increase in customer satisfaction rating for handling incidents over the next 6 months.

Metrics required:
■ Original customer satisfaction score for handling incidents
■ Ending customer satisfaction score for handling incidents.

Measurements:
■ Incident handling survey score
■ Number of survey scores.

Here is a quantitative example:
CSF: Reducing IT costs
KPI: 10 percent reduction in the costs of handling printer incidents.

Metrics required:
■ Original cost of handling printer incidents
■ Final cost of handling printer incidents
■ Cost of the improvement effort.

Measurements:
■ Time spent on the incident by first-level operative and their average salary
■ Time spent on the incident by second-level operative and their average salary
■ Time spent on problem management activities by second-level operative and their average salary
■ Time spent on the training first-level operative on the workaround
■ Cost of a service call to third-party vendor
■ Time and material from third-party vendor.

An important aspect to consider is whether a KPI is fit for use. Key questions are:
■ What does the performance indicator really tell us about goal achievement? If we fail to meet the target set for a performance indicator, does that mean we fail to achieve some of our goals? And if we succeed in meeting certain targets,

does this mean we will achieve our goals?
■ How easy is it to interpret the performance indicator? Does it help us to decide on a course of action?
■ When do we need the information? How often? How rapidly should the information be available?
■ To what extent is the performance indicator stable and accurate? Is it sensitive to external, uncontrollable influences? What amount of effort is needed for a change in result that is not marginal?
■ How easy is it to change the performance indicator itself? How easy is it to adapt the measurement system to changing circumstances or changes in our goals with respect to IT service provision?
■ To what extent can the performance indicator be measured now? Under which conditions can measurement continue? Which conditions impede measurement? Which conditions render the result meaningless?
■ Who owns this KPI? Who is responsible for collecting and analysing the data? Who is accountable for improvements based on the information?

To become acquainted with the possibilities and limitations of your measurement framework, critically review your performance indicators with the above questions in mind before you implement them.

5.2.2 Tension metrics
The effort from any support team is a balancing act of three elements:
■ Resources – people and money
■ Features – the product or service and its quality
■ The schedule.

The delivered product or service therefore represents a balanced trade-off between these three elements. Tension metrics can help create that balance by preventing teams from focusing on just one element – for example, on delivering the product or service on time. If an initiative is being driven primarily towards satisfying a business driver of on-time delivery to the exclusion of other factors, the manager will achieve this aim by flexing the resources and service features in order to meet the delivery schedule. This unbalanced focus will therefore either lead to budget increases or lower product quality. Tension metrics help create a delicate balance between shared goals and delivering a product or service according to business requirements within time and budget. Tension metrics do not, however, conflict with shared goals and values, but rather prevent teams from taking shortcuts and shirking on their assignment. Tension metrics can therefore be seen as a tool to create shared responsibilities between team members with different roles in the service lifecycle.

5.2.3 Goals and metrics

Each phase of the service lifecycle requires very specific contributions from the key roles identified in Service design, service transition and service operation, each of which has very specific goals to meet. Ultimately, the quality of the service will be determined by how well each role meets its goals, and by how well those sometimes conflicting goals are managed along the way. That makes it crucial that organizations find some way of measuring performance – by applying a set of metrics to each goal.

5.2.3.1 Breaking down goals and metrics

It is really outside the scope of this publication to dig too deeply into human resources management, and besides, there is no shortage of literature already available on the subject. However, there are some specific things that can be said about best practices for goals and metrics as they apply to managing services in their lifecycle.

Many IT service organizations measure their IT professionals on an abstract and high-level basis. During appraisal and counselling, most managers discuss such things as 'taking part in one or more projects/performing activities of a certain kind', or 'fulfilling certain roles in projects/activities' and 'following certain courses'. Although accomplishing such goals might be important for the professional growth of an individual, it does not facilitate the service lifecycle or any specific process in it. In reality, most IT service organizations do not use more detailed performance measures that are in line with key business drivers, because it is difficult to do, and do correctly.

But there is a way. In the design phase of a service, key business drivers were translated into service level requirements (SLRs) and operations level requirements, the latter consisting of process, skills and technology requirements. What this constitutes is a translation from a business requirement into requirements for IT services and IT components. There is also the question, of the strategic position of IT. In essence, the question is whether IT is an enabler or a cost centre, the answer to which determines the requirements for the IT services and IT components. The answer also determines how the processes in the service lifecycle are executed, and how the people in the organization should behave. If IT is a cost centre, services might be developed to be used centrally in order to reduce Total cost of ownership (TCO). Services will have those characteristics that will reduce total costs of ownership throughout the lifecycle. On the other hand, if IT is an enabler, services will be designed to flexibly adjust to changing business requirements and meet early time-to-market objectives.

Either way, the important point is that those requirements for IT services and IT components would determine how processes in the lifecycle are measured and managed, and thus how the performance and growth of professionals should be measured.

Best practice shows that goals and metrics can be classified into three categories: financial metrics, learning and growth metrics, and organizational or process effectiveness metrics. An example of financial metrics might be the expenses and total percentage of hours spent on projects or maintenance, while an example of learning and growth might be the percentage of education pursued in a target skill area, certification in a professional area, and contribution to knowledge management. These metrics will not be discussed in this publication.

The last type of metrics, organizational or process effectiveness metrics, can be further broken down into product quality metrics and process quality metrics. Product quality metrics are the metrics supporting the contribution to the delivery of quality products. Examples of product quality metrics are shown in the following table. Process quality metrics are the quality metrics related to efficient and effective process management.

Table 5.3 – Examples of service quality metrics [23]

Measure	Metric	Quality goal	Lower limit	Upper limit
Schedule	% variation against revised plan	Within 7.5% of estimate	Not to be less than 7.5% of estimate	Not to exceed 7.5% of estimate
Effort	% variation against revised plan	Within 10% of estimate	Not to be less than 10% of estimate	Not to exceed 10% of estimate
Cost	% variation against revised plan	Within 10% of estimate	Not to be less than 10% of estimate	Not to exceed 10% of estimate
Defects	% variation against planned defect	Within 10% of estimate	Not to be less than 10% of estimate	Not to exceed 10% of estimate
Productivity	% variation against productivity goal	Within 10% of estimate	Not to be less than 10% of estimate	Not to exceed 10% of estimate
Customer satisfaction	Customer satisfaction survey result	Greater than 8.9 on the range of 1 to 10	Not to be less than 8.9 on the range of 1 to 10	

5.2.4 Using organizational metrics

To be effective, measurements and metrics should be woven through the complete organization, touching the strategic as well as the tactical level. To successfully support the key business drivers, the IT services manager needs to know what and how well each part of the organization contributes to the final success.

It is also important, when defining measurements for goals that support the IT services strategy, to remember that measurements must focus on results and not on efforts. Focus on the organizational output and try to get clear what the contribution is. Each stage in the service lifecycle has its processes and contribution to the service. Each stage of the lifecycle also has its roles, which contribute to the development or management of the service. Based on the process goals and the quality attributes of the service, goals and metrics can be defined for each role in the processes of the lifecycle.

5.2.5 Reporting policy and rules

An ideal approach to building a business-focused service-reporting framework is to take the time to define and agree the policy and rules with the business and service design about how reporting will be implemented and managed.

This includes:

- Targeted audience(s) and the related business views on what the service delivered is
- Agreement on what to measure and what to report on

- Agreed definitions of all terms and boundaries
- Basis of all calculations
- Reporting schedules
- Access to reports and medium to be used
- Meetings scheduled to review and discuss reports.

5.2.6 Right content for the right audience

Numerous policies and rules can exist as long as it is clear for each report which policies and rules have been applied, e.g. one policy may be applied to manufacturing whereas a variant may be more suited to the sales team. However all policies and rules form part of the single reporting framework.

Once the framework, policies and rules are in place, targeting suitably styled reports becomes simply a task of translating flat historical data into meaningful business views (which can be automated). These need to be annotated around the key questions, threats, mitigations and improvements such data provoke. Reports can then be presented via the medium of choice, e.g. paper-based hard copies, online soft copies, web-enabled dynamic HTML, current snapshot whiteboards, or real-time portal/dashboards.

Simple and effective customizable and automated reporting is crucial to a successful, ongoing reporting system that is seen as adding value to the business. Over time, many of the initial standard reports may become obsolete in favour of the regular production of custom reports which have been shaped to meet changing business needs and become the standard.

The end result is the targeted recipient having clear, unambiguous and relevant information in a language and style they understand and like, accessible in the medium of their choice, and detailing the delivery of IT into their environment within their boundaries, without such information being clouded by the data related to the delivery of IT into other areas of the business. Figure 5.5 depicts the service-reporting process.

Figure 5.4 – Service reporting process [24]

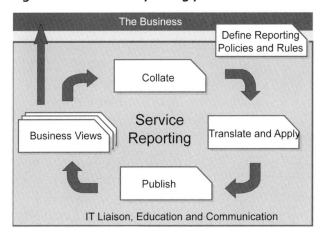

Source Continual Service Improvement was produced by OGC

5.3 BEST PRACTICES THAT SUPPORT CSI

There are many best practices, standards, models and quality systems that are in use throughout the world that support CSI in one manner or another. Previous chapters introduced some of these best practices.

5.3.1 ISO/IEC 20000

Standards make an enormous contribution, although very often that contribution is invisible. If there were no standards, it would soon be noticed. It is when there is an absence of standards that their importance is brought home. When products and services meet expectations, there is a tendency to take them for granted. Few people are usually aware of the role played by standards in raising levels of quality, safety, reliability, efficiency and interchangeability – as well as in providing such benefits at an economical cost.

ISO/IEC 20000-1:2005 defines the requirements for a service provider to deliver managed services. It may be used:

- By businesses that are going out to tender for their services
- To provide a consistent approach by all service providers in a supply chain
- To benchmark IT service management
- As the basis for an independent assessment
- To demonstrate the ability to meet customer requirements
- To improve services.

There are many aspects of ISO/IEC 20000 that support CSI but the major ones are the following.

5.3.2 Service level management

The SLM process should ensure that the service provider remains focused on the customer throughout the planning, implementing and ongoing management of service delivery. Key activities of SLM:

- Capturing initial business requirements and ongoing changes to volumes and expectations
- Defining and documenting services in a service catalogue
- Negotiating SLAs with defined targets
- Monitoring, measurement and reporting of the service levels achieved
- Initiation of corrective action
- Provide input to a SIP.

5.3.3 Service reporting

Service reports should be produced to meet identified needs and customer requirements. Service reporting should include:

- Performance against service level targets
- Non-compliance and issues such as service level or security breaches
- Workload characteristics such as volume and resource utilization
- Performance reporting following major incidents and changes
- Trend information
- Satisfaction analysis.

5.3.4 Business relationship management

- The objective of business relationship management is to establish and maintain a good relationship between the service provider and the customer based on understanding the customer and their business **drivers**. The **customer** business drivers could require changes in SLAs and thus becomes input into service improvement opportunities.

■ The objective of **supplier management** is to ensure the provision of seamless, quality services. This will require monitoring, measuring and reviewing the performance of IT suppliers.

Management decisions and corrective actions should take into consideration the findings in the service reports and should be formally communicated.

ISO/IEC 20000 defines a requirement for continual improvement on the **effectiveness** and **efficiency** of service delivery and management. This is done through management establishing policies, objectives and the need for continual improvement. ISO follows the **Plan-Do-Check-Act** cycle. Checking involves monitoring, measuring and analysing, and acting is the continual improvement.

5.3.5 COBIT®

Control OBjectives for Information and Related Technology (COBIT) is a globally recognized and adopted controls-based, value and **risk management** framework used to support overall IT **governance**. COBIT is a flexible framework that needs to be aligned to an organization's business requirements. It can be used by management, consultants and auditors to:

■ Define the IT **controls** needed to minimize risks and add business value – and hence the development of a fit-for-purpose IT governance framework

■ Create an IT measurement and CSI framework which is aligned to the business goals for IT

■ Assess and **audit** against IT governance and ensure that IT governance aligns with overall enterprise governance.

■ COBIT supports CSI in three ways:

■ COBIT defines processes to support CSI

■ COBIT provides **maturity models** that can be used to **benchmark** and drive CSI

■ COBIT provides goals and **metrics** aligned to the business goals for IT, which can be used to create an IT management **dashboard**.

5.3.5.1 COBIT defines processes to support CSI

COBIT has defined four **processes** needed to support CSI. The COBIT process domain 'Monitor and evaluate' (ME) defines the processes needed to assess current IT **performance**, IT **controls** and regulatory **compliance**. The processes are:

■ ME1: Monitor and evaluate IT performance

■ ME2: Monitor and evaluate internal control

■ ME3: Ensure regulatory compliance

■ ME4: Provide IT governance.

These processes take into consideration multiple factors that can drive the need for improvement, factors such as a need to improve performance and manage risks more effectively through better controls or regulatory compliance. These processes also ensure that any improvement actions are identified and managed through to their implementation.

An enterprise can therefore implement the processes needed to support CSI using COBIT processes. In addition, an enterprise can review the processes that support CSI periodically and improve them based on their associated **maturity** models within COBIT.

5.3.6 Six Sigma

Six Sigma is an IT-appropriate process-improvement methodology, though the fundamental **objective** is to reduce **errors** to fewer than 3.4 defects per million executions (regardless of the process). Given the wide variation in IT **deliverables** (e.g. **change management**, **problem management**, **capacity management**) and **roles** and tasks within IT operational **environments**, IT managers must determine whether it is reasonable to expect delivery at a Six Sigma level.

Six Sigma is a data-driven approach that supports continual improvement. It is business output driven in relation to customer **specification** and focuses on dramatically reducing process variation using statistical **process control** (SPC) measures.

Six Sigma's objective is the implementation of a measurement-oriented **strategy** focused on process improvement and defects reduction. A Six Sigma defect is defined as anything outside customer specifications.

There are two primary sub-methodologies within Six Sigma: DMAIC (define, measure, analyse, improve, control) and DMADV (define, measure, analyse, **design**, verify). The DMAIC process is an improvement method for existing processes for which performance does not meet expectations, or for which incremental improvements are desired. The DMADV process focuses on the creation of new processes.

Defining, measuring and analysing are key activities of CSI.

Since Six Sigma requires data it is important to start capturing data as soon as possible. As previously mentioned if the data is questionable, this is not a **problem** as it provides the opportunity to analyse why the data doesn't make sense.

5.3.7 CMMI

capability maturity model integration (CMMI) is a process improvement approach that provides organizations with the essential elements of effective process measurement. It can be used to guide process improvement across a **project**, a division or an entire **organization**. CMMI helps integrate traditionally separate organizational functions, sets process improvement goals and priorities, provides guidance for **quality** processes and provides a point of reference for appraising current processes.

CMMI uses a hierarchy of five levels, each with a progressively greater **capability** of producing quality, where each level is described as a level of maturity.

5.3.7.1 CMMI Benefits

CMMI **best practices** enable organizations to do the following:

- More explicitly link management and engineering activities to their **business objectives**

- Expand the **scope** of and visibility into the product life cycle and engineering activities to ensure that the product or **service** meets customer expectations

- Incorporate lessons learned from additional areas of best practice (e.g. measurement, **risk management** and **supplier management**)

- Implement more robust, high-maturity **practices**

- Address additional organizational functions critical to their products and **services**

- More fully comply with relevant ISO **standards**.

5.3.8 Project management

It is also important to understand that a structured project management method, such as PMI (Project Management Institute) or **PRINCE2 (PRojects IN Controlled Environments**, v2) can be used when improving **IT services**. Not all improvements will require a structured **project** approach, but many will, due to the sheer scope and scale of the improvement.

Project management is discussed in great detail in the **ITIL Service Transition** volume.

5.3.8.1 Gantt chart

Henry Gantt (1861–1919) created the Gantt chart in a setting and time which was deeply involved in exploring **efficiency** in manufacturing, time and motion studies, and the formulation of 'scientific management' (the foundation of modern management principals). Today many people see the Gantt chart as a project management tool, however its origins are completely intertwined with **process**.

Gantt charts use time-lengthened bars to represent tasks. Tasks are connected to each other according to predecessors and dependencies. Simple arrows are used to connect the task bars. See Figure 5.5.

The simplicity of the Gantt chart makes it easy to use and read. It is especially legible to project managers and staff often engaged in project based work. It has been successfully used on highly complex **projects** such as the building of the Hoover Dam and the creation of the interstate highway network in the US. Its limitations are its inability to show organizational/ departmental structures associated with tasks, an inability to include process/workflow rules, and inabilities to show split and join actions.

5.3.8.2 Rummler-Brache Swim Lane

Process Swim Lanes were first described in Geary Rummler and Alan Brache's publication Improving Performance. Their **impact** in the process world is difficult to overstate. Their work has focused on helping companies improve their overall **business processes**, and thereby become more competitive and profitable. Process Swim Lanes have become the most ubiquitous term and method associated with their names.

Figure 5.5 – Gantt chart[25]

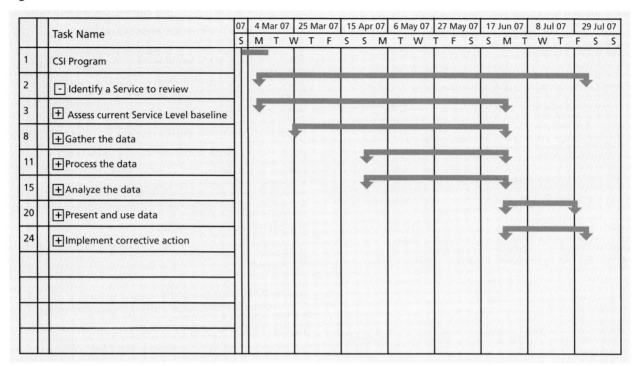

Source Continual Service Improvement was produced by OGC

It is a highly effective way to display the **relationship** between processes and organizations/ departments. Swim Lanes are essentially flow charts which include horizontal or vertical bands to include customers, departments and technology.

Swim Lanes rely on rectangles for activities/tasks, decision diamonds, and arrows to represent flow. Central to the method is separating organizations with horizontal rows.

Each **activity** is placed in the row (Swim Lane) which represents the organization responsible for completing the task. See Figure 5.6.

Swim Lanes are strong tools for communicating with business managers. Many managers are essentially organizational thinkers. They see the world in organizational terms. In the absence of those structures they will sometimes struggle. Swim Lanes describe a process from a viewpoint which is familiar and accessible.

The weakness of Swim Lanes stems from the fact that it is more of an approach than a standard. Managing complexity is generally done by including symbols from other standards within a Swim Lane diagram.

Figure 5.6 – Rummler-Brache Swim Lane example[26]

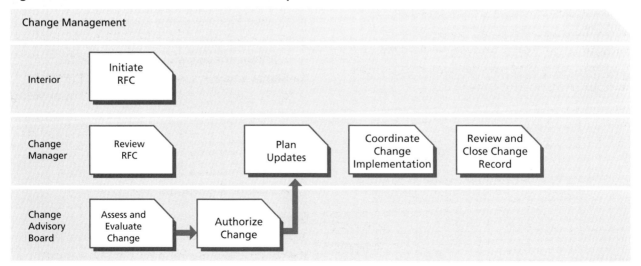

Source Continual Service Improvement was produced by OGC

5.3.8.3 Value Stream Mapping

Value Stream Mapping is a hands-on method which comes from Lean Manufacturing (an approach to removing non-value-added work – originating with Toyota). It is traditionally a facilitation method done on whiteboards or on paper. The result is often a handmade, somewhat cartoonish representation of how a product is produced from inception to delivery to the customer. It includes process, information flow and a timeline separating value-add and non-value-add activities.

Value Stream Maps include handmade drawings for all types of mechanisms within the process: factories, trucks, people, documents, tasks etc. It is by its nature an eclectic and ad hoc method of diagramming a process.

Value Stream Mapping is a good tool for projects whose goal is to streamline a process. It ensures a high-level view which is broad and customer focused. It is not generally used as a tool for long-term documentation, but instead as a method of setting the right direction and staying on track. It can be a powerful tool when combined with other diagramming standards such as BPMN or IDEF. It is not a standard and as such does not have rigidity required for long-term documentation.

5.3.9 Total quality management

Total quality management (TQM) is a management strategy aimed at embedding awareness of quality in all organizational processes.

TQM is a set of systematic activities carried out by the entire organization to effectively and efficiently achieve company objectives so as to provide products and services with a level of quality that satisfies customers, at the appropriate time and price.

At the core of TQM is a management approach to long-term success through customer satisfaction. In a TQM effort, all members of an organization participate in improving processes, products, services and the culture in which they work.

Quality management for IT services is a systematic way of ensuring that all the activities necessary to design, develop and implement IT services which satisfy the requirements of the organization and of users take place as planned and that the activities are carried out cost-effectively.

The way that an organization plans to manage its operations so that it delivers quality services is specified by its quality management system. The quality management system defines the organizational structure, responsibilities, policies, procedures, processes, standards and resources required to deliver quality IT services. However, a quality management system will only function as intended if management and staff are committed to achieving its objectives. This section gives brief details on a number of different quality approaches.

5.3.9.1 Deming Cycle

The Deming Cycle of Plan-Do-Check-Act is an effective quality management system to follow. A core concept in implementing TQM is Deming's 14 points, a set of management practices to help companies increase their quality and productivity:

1 Create constancy of purpose for improving products and services.
2 Adopt the new philosophy.
3 Cease dependence on inspection to achieve quality.
4 End the practice of awarding business on price alone; instead, minimize total cost by working with a single supplier.
5 Improve constantly and forever every process for planning, production and service.
6 Institute training on the job.
7 Adopt and institute leadership.
8 Drive out fear.
9 Break down barriers between staff areas.
10 Eliminate slogans, exhortations and targets for the workforce.
11 Eliminate numerical quotas for the workforce and numerical goals for management.
12 Remove barriers that rob people of pride of workmanship, and eliminate the annual rating or merit system.
13 Institute a vigorous programme of education and self-improvement for everyone.
14 Put everybody in the company to work accomplishing the transformation.

5.3.9.2 Juran

Joseph Juran became a recognized name in the quality field in 1951 with the publication of the *Quality Control Handbook*. The appeal was to the Japanese initially, and Juran was asked to give a series of lectures in 1954 on **planning**, organizational issues, management responsibility for quality, and the need to set goals and targets for improvement. Juran devised a well-known chart, 'The Juran Trilogy', shown in Table 5.4, to represent the relationship between quality planning, quality control and quality improvement on a project-by-project basis.

A further feature of Juran's approach is the recognition of the need to guide managers; this is achieved by the establishment of a quality council within an organization, which is responsible for establishing **processes**, nominating projects, assigning teams, making improvements and providing the necessary resources.

5.3.9.3 The Quality Trilogy
Senior management plays a key role in serving on the quality council, approving strategic goals, allocating resources and **reviewing** progress. Juran promotes a four-phased approach to **quality** improvement, shown in Table 5.4.

Table 5.4 – Juran's four-phased approach[27]

Start-up:	creating the necessary organizational structures and infrastructure
Test:	in which concepts are tried out in **pilot** programmes and results evaluated
Scale-up:	in which the basic concepts are extended based on positive feedback
Institutionalization:	at which point quality improvements are linked to the strategic business **plan**.

Source Continual Service Improvement was produced by OGC

5.3.9.4 Crosby
The Crosby TQM approach is very popular in the UK. The approach is based on Crosby's Four Absolutes of Quality Management:

- Quality is conformance to **requirement**.
- The system for causing quality is prevention and not appraisal.
- The **performance** standard must be zero defects and not 'that's close enough'.
- The measure of quality is the price of non-conformance and not indices.

The Crosby approach is often based on familiar slogans; however, **organizations** may experience difficulty in translating the quality messages into sustainable methods of quality improvement. Some organizations have found it difficult to integrate their quality initiatives, having placed their quality **programme** outside the mainstream management process.

Anecdotal evidence suggests that these pitfalls result in difficulties being experienced in sustaining active **quality** campaigns over a number of years in some organizations.

5.3.10 Management governance framework
The management **governance** framework and its processes are the means by which: 'A business directs, develops and delivers the products and **services** of the business.'

It is the way that the **strategy** is executed through business development products to develop product and service capabilities and through which day-to-day products and services are delivered and supported. It is the mechanism by which all the parts of the business and its **supply chain** partners work together on strategy, **development** and **operation**.

Figure 5.7 illustrates the framework and what is involved in it. The framework is used to direct and run the business from left to right with feedback from right to left. Typically the strategy involves a long-term strategy; the business plan involves a short number of years with financial targets and budgets; the business architecture is the high-level design of the business, and so on.

The business needs to provide unified direction through disciplines and processes that involve strategy, business plans, budgets and business architecture.

The business needs to provide unified development through a shared business change **plan** and development programmes and **projects** disciplines under the control of operational change disciplines in the operational world.

The business needs to provide unified delivery of products and services through shared operational planning, operational delivery and operational support. The way the disciplines above are performed varies from business to business. Some

Figure 5.7 Management governance framework [28]

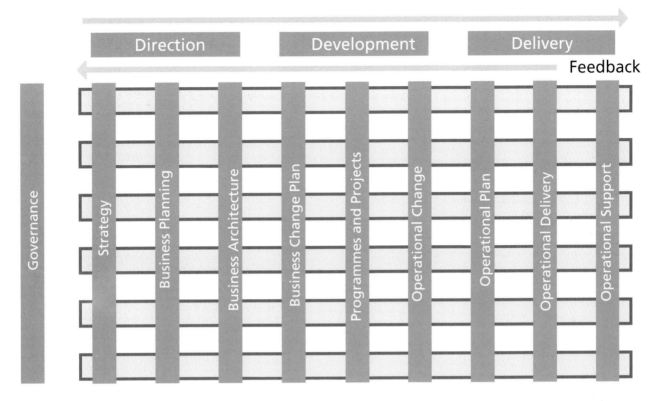

Source Continual Service Improvement was produced by OGC

businesses perform aspects formally and other aspects in an informal, ad hoc manner. In terms of best-practice business governance, the need for the individual disciplines above is crucial as is the way they interrelate. The governance framework formalizes the touch points between the value chains. From both business and IT viewpoints, the best-practice governance framework enables the processes and the relationships of the value chains to be formalized with each other across the governance model.

5.4 CHALLENGES, CRITICAL SUCCESS FACTORS AND RISKS

The major challenge facing the service catalogue management process is that of maintaining an accurate service catalogue as part of a service portfolio, incorporating both the business service catalogue and the technical service catalogue as part of an overall CMS and SKMS. This is best approached by developing stand-alone spreadsheets or databases before trying to integrate the service catalogue and service portfolio within the CMS or SKMS. In order to achieve this, the culture of the organization needs to accept that the catalogue and portfolio are

essential sources of information that everyone within the IT organization needs to use and help maintain. This will often assist in the standardization of the service catalogue and the service portfolio and enable increase in cost performance through economies of scale.

The main critical success factors for the service catalogue management process are:

■ An accurate service catalogue

■ Business users' awareness of the services being provided

■ IT staff awareness of the technology supporting the services.

The risks associated with the provision of an accurate service catalogue are:

■ Inaccuracy of the data in the catalogue and it not being under rigorous change control

■ Poor acceptance of the service catalogue and its usage in all operational processes. The more active the catalogue is, the more likely it is to be accurate in its content

■ Inaccuracy of information received from the business, IT and the service portfolio, with regard to service information

- The tools and resources required to maintain the information
- Poor access to accurate change management information and processes
- Poor access to and support of appropriate and up-to-date CMS and SKMS
- Circumvention of the use of the service portfolio and service catalogue
- The information is either too detailed to maintain accurately or at too high a level to be of any value. It should be consistent with the level of detail within the CMS and the SKMS.

SECTION 6 – THE BUSINESS CASE

SCM:06

Traditionally, IT has completed Business Cases and used them as a decisions support tool. Capturing qualitative and quantitative information, the Business Case has value for the business that traditionally funds IT projects and benefits for IT that traditionally implement IT projects.

When considering finance, the Return on Investment (ROI) is the ratio of money gained or lost relative to money invested. Obtaining funding and justifying activities within IT organizations often requires creation of a plan or document defining the expected investments and returns. Called a Business Case, this document or set of documents is the justification for a significant item of expenditure, including a Service Catalogue. A Business Case includes information about costs, benefits, options, issues, risks, and possible problems.

ITIL v3 introduces important guidance regarding a sound Business Case, and a model capturing five major sections of a sound Business Case. Understanding the key Business Case elements of Introduction, Methods and Assumptions, Business Impacts, Risks and Contingencies, and Recommendations provides a rigorous framework to justify and validate investment decisions.

Understanding how a Service Catalogue and its related business objectives is influenced by Business Case elements can be a major contributor to setting expectations and benchmarks for success. In particular, the Business Impacts expected are often critical drivers of expectations and measures of success.

Researching and considering the contributors to the Business Case, including roles across IT and the business and current and expected demand, help drive Service Strategy and bridge Service Operation, Service Design and Financial Management. A Business Case is an important concept in developing a marketing mentality and focusing on facilitating business value.

This section investigates the key components in the creation of a Business Case for Service Catalogue, and details its major sections and influences.

6.1 The five major sections of a business case

Table 6.1 – Sample business case structure [29]

Business case structure	
A.	**Introduction** Presents the business objectives addressed by the service
B.	**Methods and assumptions** Defines the boundaries of the business case, such as time period, whose costs and whose benefits
C.	**Business impacts** The financial and non-financial business case results
D.	**Risks and contingencies** The probability that alternative results will emerge
E.	**Recommendations** Specific actions recommended.

Source Service Design was produced by OGC

6.2 Business objectives

The structure of a business case varies from organization to organization. A generic form is given in Table 6.1. What they all have in common is a detailed analysis of business impact or benefits. Business impact is in turn linked to business objectives. A business objective is the reason for considering a service management initiative in the first place. Objectives should start broadly. For example:

■ The business objectives for commercial provider organizations are usually the objectives of the business itself, including financial and organizational performance.

■ The business objectives for not-for-profit organizations are usually the objectives for the constituents, population or membership served as well as financial and organizational performance.

Table 6.2 illustrates possible business objectives.

Table 6.2 – Common business objectives [30]

Operational	Financial	Strategic	Industry
Shorten **development** time	Improve return on **assets**	Establish or enhance **strategic** positioning	Increase market share
Increase productivity	Avoid costs	Introduce competitive products	Improve market position
Increase **capacity**	Increase discretionary spending as a percentage of **budget**	Improve professionalism of **organization**	Increase repeat business
Increase **reliability**	Decrease non-discretionary spending	Improve customer satisfaction	Take market leadership
Minimize **risks**	Increase revenues	Provide better **quality**	Recognized as producer of reliable or **quality** products or services
Improve **resource** utilization	Increase margins	Provide customized offerings	Recognized as low price leader
Improve efficiencies	Keep spending to within budget	Introduce new products or services	Recognized as compliant to industry standards

Source Service Strategy was produced by OGC

6.2.1 Business impact

While most of a **business case** argument relies on **cost** analysis, there is much more to a service management initiative than financials. The **scope** of possible non-financial business **impacts** is summarized in this way: a **business** impact has no value unless it is linked to a **business objective**. There need not be a one-to-one **relationship** between business impact and business objective. Examples are given in Figures 6.1 and 6.2.

Figure 6.1 – Single business impact can affect multiple business objectives [31]

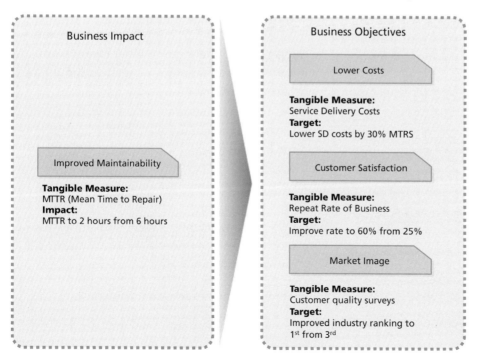

Source Service Strategy was produced by OGC

Figure 6.2 – Multiple business impacts can affect a single business objective [32]

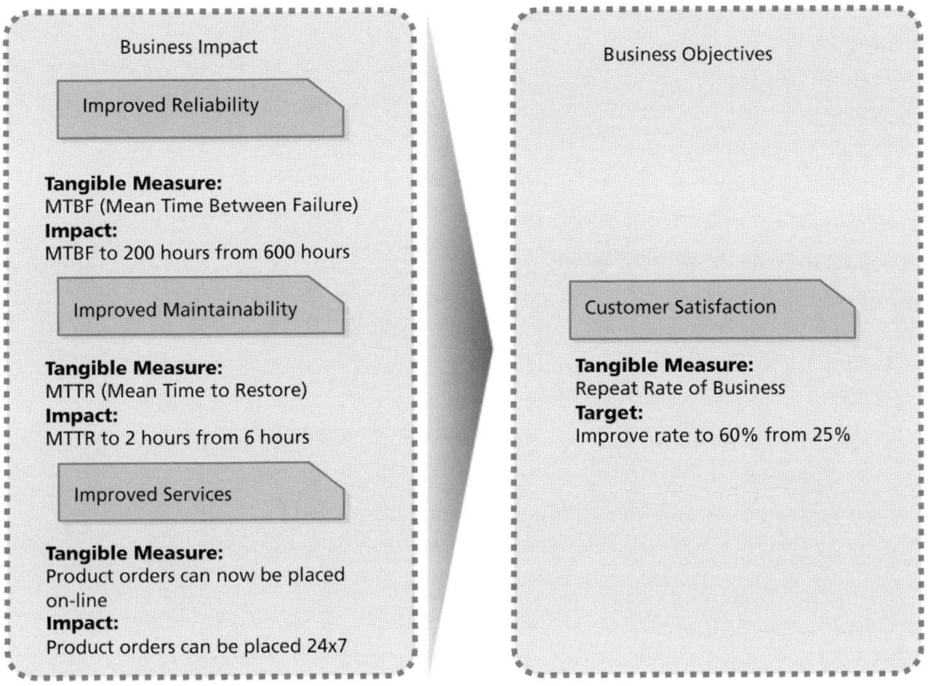

Business Impact

Improved Reliability

Tangible Measure:
MTBF (Mean Time Between Failure)
Impact:
MTBF to 200 hours from 600 hours

Improved Maintainability

Tangible Measure:
MTTR (Mean Time to Restore)
Impact:
MTTR to 2 hours from 6 hours

Improved Services

Tangible Measure:
Product orders can now be placed
on-line
Impact:
Product orders can be placed 24x7

Business Objectives

Customer Satisfaction

Tangible Measure:
Repeat Rate of Business
Target:
Improve rate to 60% from 25%

*Source Service Strategy
was produced by OGC*

It is easy for a business case to focus on financial analysis and neglect non-financial impacts. The end result is a business case that is not as convincing as it should be. By incorporating business impacts linked to business objectives, a business case is more compelling.

6.3 Contributors to the business case

6.3.1 Organization

Organization assets are active configurations of people, processes, applications and infrastructure that carry out all organizational activity through the principles of specialization and coordination. This category of assets includes the functional hierarchies, social networks of groups, teams and individuals, as well as the systems they use to work together towards shared goals and incentives. Organization assets include the patterns that people, applications, information and infrastructure deploy, either by design or by self-adaptive process, to maximize the creation of value for stakeholders. Some service organizations are superior to others simply by virtue of organization. For example, networks of wireless access points, storage systems, point-of-sale terminals, databases, hardware stores and remote backup facilities. Strategic location of assets by itself is a basis for superior performance and competitive advantage.

See over for figure.

Figure 6.3 – Product Managers have a key role under Service Portfolio Management[33]

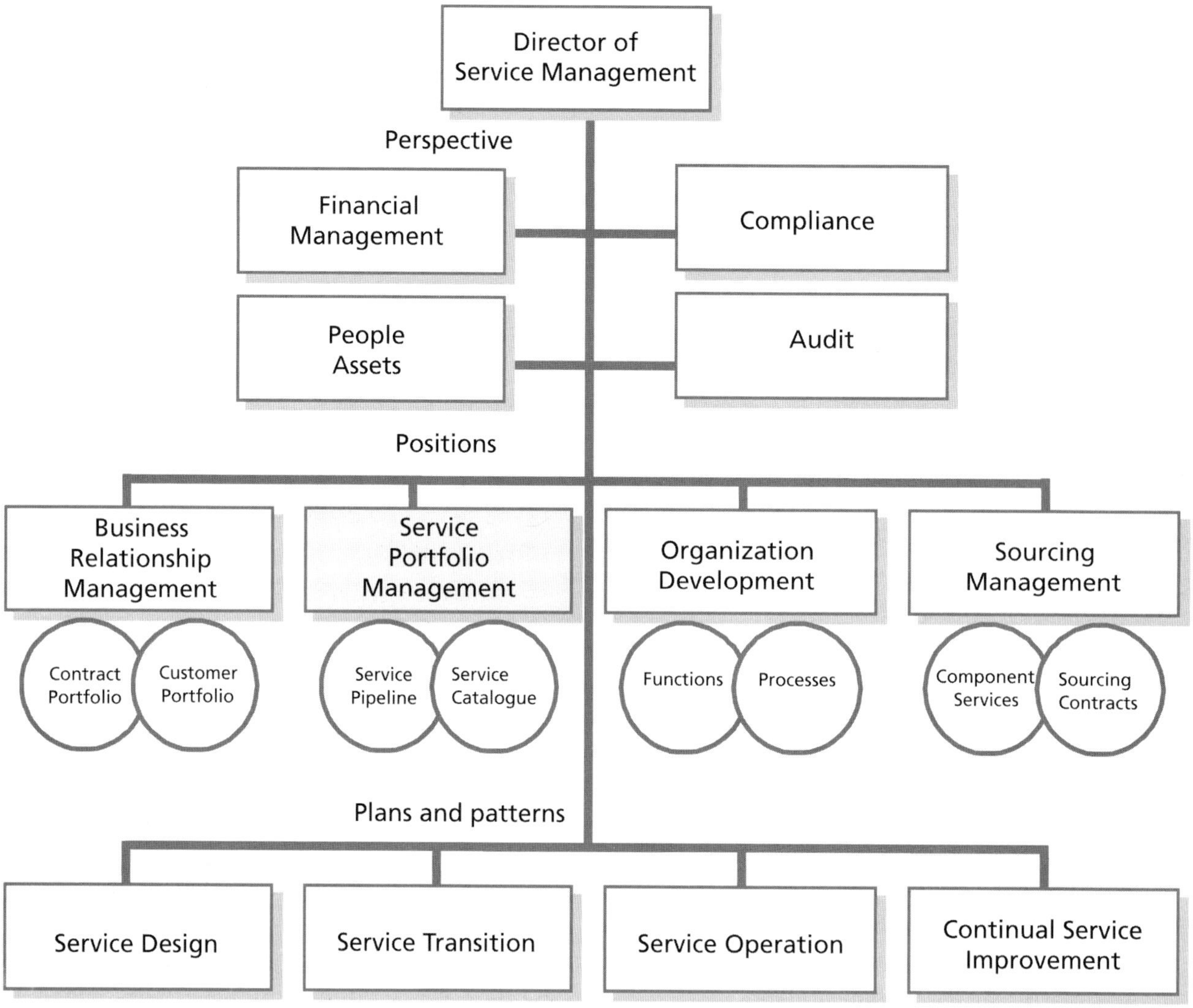

Source Service Strategy was produced by OGC

SECTION 7 – KEY RELATIONSHIPS & TOUCH POINTS

SCM:07

The Service Catalogue Management processes, as well as the Service Catalogue technology implementation, operate within a complex system that spans multiple lifecycle processes and functions. As the "spine" of ITIL v3, Service Catalogue success requires several critical associations and interactions.

Considering automation and the ITIL v3 Request Fulfilment process in the implementation of a Service Catalogue can improve service quality and responsiveness. As users request services and IT fulfils these requests, patterns of demand as well as costs automatically compute. Where appropriate, automation can, in many cases, provide payback that can offset the cost of acquisition of the technology. This automation provides dividends in terms of managing assets and potentially provisioning them as well.

The value proposition of Service Catalogue includes automation of routine tasks through Request Fulfilment, as well as enhancing Asset and Configuration Management, augmenting access controls, documenting demands for services and developing data for Financial Management.

This unit explores how a Service Catalogue Management process spans multiple ITIL v3 processes, and how an effective Service Catalogue contributes vital financial, market and design information.

7.1   REQUEST FULFILMENT

The term 'service request' is used as a generic description for many varying types of demands that are placed upon the IT department by the users. Many of these are actually small changes – low risk, frequently occurring, low cost, etc. (e.g. a request to change a password, a request to install an additional software application onto a particular workstation, a request to relocate some items of desktop equipment) or maybe just a question requesting information – but their scale and frequent, low-risk nature means that they are better handled by a separate process, rather than being allowed to congest and obstruct the normal incident and change management processes.

7.1.1   Purpose/goal/objective

Request fulfilment is the process of dealing with service requests from the users. The objectives of the request fulfilment process include:

- To provide a channel for users to request and receive standard services for which a pre-defined approval and qualification process exists
- To provide information to users and customers about the availability of services and the procedure for obtaining them
- To source and deliver the components of requested standard services (e.g. licences and software media)
- To assist with general information, complaints or comments.
- Process activities, methods and techniques
- Menu selection

Request fulfilment offers great opportunities for self-help practices where users can generate a service request using technology that links into service management tools. Ideally, users should be offered a 'menu'-type selection via a web interface, so that they can select and input details of service requests from a pre-defined list –where appropriate expectations can be set by giving target delivery and/or implementation targets/dates (in line with SLA targets). Where organizations are offering a self-help IT support capability to the users, it would make sense to combine this with a request fulfilment system as described.

Specialist web tools to offer this type of 'shopping basket' experience can be used together with interfaces directly to the back-end integrated ITSM tools, or other more general business process automation or enterprise resource planning (ERP) tools that may be used for management of the request fulfilment activities.

7.1.2   Challenges, critical success factors and risks

7.1.2.1   Challenges

The following challenges will be faced when introducing request fulfilment:

- Clearly defining and documenting the type of requests that will be handled within the request fulfilment process (and those that will either go through the service desk and be handled as incidents or those that will need to go through formal change management) – so that all parties are absolutely clear on the scope.

- Establishing self-help front-end capabilities that allow the users to interface successfully with the request fulfilment process.

7.1.2.2 Critical success factors

Request fulfilment depends on the following critical success factors:

- Agreement of what services will be standardized and who is authorized to request them. The cost of these services must also be agreed. This may be done as part of the SLM process. Any variances of the services must also be defined.

- Publication of the services to users as part of the service catalogue. It is important that this part of the service catalogue must be easily accessed, perhaps on the intranet, and should be recognized as the first source of information for users seeking access to a service.

- Definition of a standard fulfilment procedure for each of the services being requested. This includes all procurement policies and the ability to generate purchase orders and work orders

- A single point of contact which can be used to request the service. This is often provided by the service desk or through an intranet request, but could be through an automated request directly into the request fulfilment or procurement system.

- Self-service tools needed to provide a front-end interface to the users. It is essential that these integrate with the back-end fulfilment tools, often managed through incident or change management.

7.2 ACCESS MANAGEMENT

Access management is the process of granting authorized users the right to use a service, while preventing access to non-authorized users. It has also been referred to as rights management or identity management in different organizations.

7.2.1 Policies/principles/basic concepts

Access management is the process that enables users to use the services that are documented in the service catalogue. It comprises the following basic concepts:

- Access refers to the level and extent of a service's functionality or data that a user is entitled to use.

- Identity refers to the information about them that distinguishes them as an individual and which verifies their status within the organization. By definition, the identity of a user is unique to that user. (This is covered in more detail in paragraph 4.5.7.1.)

- Rights (also called privileges) refer to the actual settings whereby a user is provided access to a service or group of services. Typical rights, or levels of access, include read, write, execute, change, delete.

- Services or service groups. Most users do not use only one service, and users performing a similar set of activities will use a similar set of services. Instead of providing access to each service for each user separately, it is more efficient to be able to grant each user – or group of users – access to the whole set of services that they are entitled to use at the same time.

- Directory services refers to a specific type of tool that is used to manage access and rights.

7.2.2 Process activities, methods and techniques

7.2.2.1 Requesting access

Access (or restriction) can be requested using one of any number of mechanisms, including:

- A standard request generated by the human resource system. This is generally done whenever a person is hired, promoted, transferred or when they leave the company

- A request for change

- A service request submitted via the request fulfilment system

- By executing a pre-authorized script or option (e.g. downloading an application from a staging server as and when it is needed).

Rules for requesting access are normally documented as part of the service catalogue.

7.2.3 Triggers, input and output/ inter-process interfaces

Access management is triggered by a request for a user or users to access a service or group of services. This could originate from any of the following:

- **An RFC**. This is most frequently used for large-scale service introductions or upgrades where the **rights** of a significant number of users need to be updated as part of the **project**.

- A **service request**. This is usually initiated through the **service desk**, or directly into the **request fulfilment system**, and executed by the relevant technical or **application management** teams.

- A request from the appropriate **human resources management** personnel (which should be channelled via the **service desk**). This is usually generated as part of the process for hiring, promoting, relocating and termination or retirement.

- A request from the **manager of a department**, who could be performing an HR role, or who could have made a decision to start using a service for the first time.

Access management should be linked to the human resource processes to verify the **user's** identify as well as to ensure that they are entitled to the services being requested.

Information security management is a key **driver** for access management as it will provide the **security** and data protection policies and tools needed to execute access management.

Change management plays an important **role** as the means to **control** the actual requests for access. This is because any request for access to a service is a **change**, although it is usually processed as a **standard change** or **service request** (possibly using a **model**) once the criteria for access have been agreed through SLM.

SLM maintains the **agreements** for access to each **service**. This will include the criteria for who is entitled to access each service, what the **cost** of that access will be, if appropriate and what level of access will be granted to different types of user (e.g. managers or staff).

There is also a strong **relationship** between access management and **configuration management**.

The CMS can be used for data storage and interrogated to determine current access details.

7.3 SERVICE ASSET AND CONFIGURATION MANAGEMENT

7.3.1 Basic concepts

7.3.1.1 The configuration model

Configuration management delivers a **model** of the services, assets and the infrastructure by recording the **relationships** between **configuration items** as shown in Figure 7.1. This enables other processes to access valuable information, e.g.:

- To assess the **impact** and cause of **incidents** and **problems**

- To assess the impact of proposed changes

- To plan and **design** new or changed services

- To plan technology refresh and software upgrades

- To plan **release** and **deployment** packages and migrate **service assets** to different locations and service centres

- To **optimize** asset utilization and costs, e.g. consolidate data centres, reduce variations and re-use assets.

The real power of configuration management's logical model of the services and infrastructure is that it is THE model – a single common representation used by all parts of IT service management, and beyond, such as HR, finance, supplier and customers.

'Danish clock'

There is a traditional Danish proverb that runs 'When you have a clock in your house, you know the time – once you get two clocks you are no longer certain.' SACM delivers that one clock for all processes and so glues them together, delivers consistency and helps achieve common purpose. (From Hans Dithmar)

The configuration items and related configuration information can be at varying levels of detail, e.g. an overview of all the services or a detailed level to view the **specification** for a service **component**.

Configuration management should be applied at a more detailed level where the **service provider** requires tight **control**, traceability and tight

Figure 7.1 – Example of a logical configuration model [34]

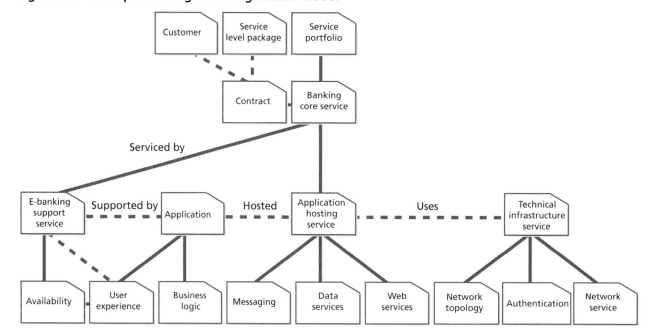

Source Service Transition was produced by OGC

coupling of configuration information through the service lifecycle.

7.3.1.2 Configuration items

A **configuration item** (CI) is an **asset**, service **component** or other item that is, or will be, under the **control** of configuration management. Configuration items may vary widely in complexity, size and type, ranging from an entire **service** or **system** including all hardware, software, documentation and support staff to a single software module or a minor hardware component. Configuration items may be grouped and managed together, e.g. a set of components may be grouped into a **release**. Configuration items should be selected using established selection criteria, grouped, classified and identified in such a way that they are manageable and traceable throughout the service **lifecycle**.

There will be a variety of CIs; the following categories may help to identify them.

- **Service lifecycle CIs** such as the **business case**, **service management plans**, service lifecycle plans, **service design package**, release and change plans, and **test** plans. They provide a picture of the service provider's services, how these services will be delivered, what benefits are expected, at what **cost**, and when they will be realized.
- **Service CIs** such as:

  - Service **capability** assets: management, **organization**, processes, knowledge, people
  - Service **resource** assets: financial capital, systems, **applications**, information, data, infrastructure and facilities, financial capital, people
  - Service **model**
  - Service **package**
  - Release package
  - **Service acceptance criteria**.

- **Organization CIs** – Some documentation will define the characteristics of a CI whereas other documentation will be a CI in its own right and need to be controlled, e.g. the organization's **business** strategy or other policies that are internal to the organization but independent of the **service provider**. Regulatory or statutory **requirements** also form external products that need to be tracked, as do products shared between more than one group.

- **Internal CIs** comprising those delivered by individual **projects**, including tangible (data centre) and intangible assets such as software that are required to deliver and maintain the service and infrastructure.

- **External CIs** such as **external customer requirements** and **agreements**, **releases** from **suppliers** or sub-contractors and external services.

■ **Interface CI**s that are required to deliver the end-to-end **service** across a **service provider interface** (SPI).

7.3.1.3 Configuration management system

To manage large and complex **IT services** and infrastructures, **service asset and configuration management** requires the use of a supporting **system** known as the **configuration management system** (CMS).

The CMS holds all the information for CIs within the designated **scope**. Some of these items will have related **specifications** or files that contain the contents of the item, e.g. software, **document** or photograph. For example, a Service CI will include the details such as supplier, **cost**, purchase date and renewal date for licences and maintenance **contracts** and the related documentation such as SLAs and **underpinning contracts**.

The CMS is also used a for wide range of purposes, for example asset data held in the CMS may be made available to external financial

asset management systems to perform specific asset management processes reporting outside of **configuration management**.

The CMS maintains the **relationships** between all service **components** and any related **incidents**, **problems**, **known errors**, change and release documentation and may also contain corporate data about employees, suppliers, locations and **business units**, customers and **users**.

Figure 4.8 shows how the CMS covers the data and information layers of the data/information/knowledge hierarchy explained in the ITIL v3 Service Transition book, section 4.7, **Knowledge Management**.

At the data level, the CMS may take data from several physical CMDBs, which together constitute a federated CMDB. Other data sources will also plug into the CMS such as the definitive media libraries. The CMS will provide access to data in asset inventories wherever possible rather than duplicating data.

Figure 7.2 Example of a Configuration Management System [35]

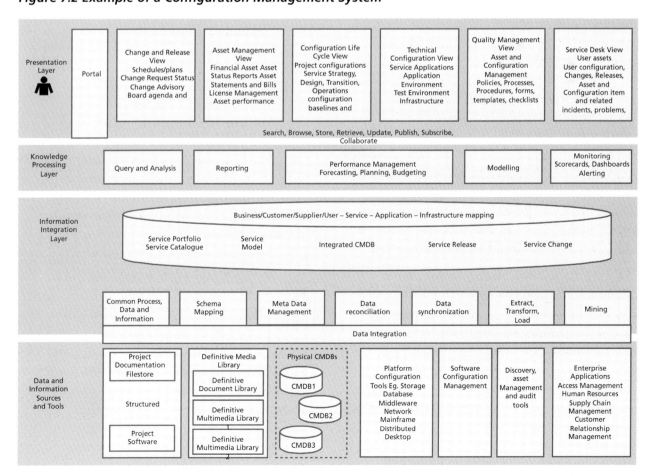

Source Service Transition was produced by OGC

Example of multiple configuration management databases

In the commonly encountered partially outsourced **service provider**, some elements of the **service management** will be outsourced while others will remain in house, and different elements may be outsourced to different external suppliers. For example the network and hardware support may be handled by supplier A, **environment** and **facilities management** by supplier B, and multiple applications suppliers and incident management handled internally. The **service desk** will access information to assist them from the CMS, but that **system** will derive its data input from discrete repositories – each one a CMDB – owned and maintained by the three parties but working together to supply a single consistent information set.

Configuration information evolves as the service is developed through the service **lifecycle**. Often there are separate mechanisms for managing different service lifecycle stages as well as different means of managing different **applications** and platforms.

7.3.1.4 Example of a configuration management system

The CMS typically contains configuration data and information that combined into an integrated set of views for different **stakeholders** through the service lifecycle as illustrated in Figure 4.8. It therefore needs to be based on appropriate web, reporting and database technologies that provide flexible and powerful visualization and mapping tools, interrogation and reporting facilities.

Many organizations are already using some elements of SACM, often maintaining **records** in **documents**, spreadsheets or local databases, and some of these may be used in the overall CMS.

Automated processes to load and update the **configuration management database** should be developed where possible so as to reduce **errors** and **optimize** costs. Discovery tools, inventory and audit tools, enterprise **systems** and network management tools can be interfaced to the CMS. These tools can be used initially to populate a CMDB, and subsequently to compare the actual 'live' configuration with the information and records stored in the CMS.

7.3.1.5 Secure libraries and secure stores

A secure library is a collection of software, electronic or **document** CIs of known type and **status**. Access to items in a secure library is restricted. Libraries are used for controlling and releasing **components** throughout the service **lifecycle**, e.g. in **design**, building, testing, **deployment** and operations.

A secure store is a location that warehouses IT **assets**. It is identified within SACM, e.g. secure stores used for desktop deployment. Secure stores play an important **role** in the provision of **security** and continuity – maintaining reliable access to equipment of known **quality**.

7.3.1.6 The definitive media library

The **definitive media library** (DML) is the secure library in which the definitive authorized **versions** of all media CIs are stored and protected. It stores master copies of versions that have passed quality assurance checks. This library may in reality consist of one or more software libraries or file-storage areas, separate from **development**, **test** or live file-store areas. It contains the master copies of all controlled software in an **organization**. The DML should include definitive copies of purchased software (along with licence documents or information), as well as software developed on site. Master copies of controlled documentation for a **system** are also stored in the DML in electronic form.

The DML will also include a physical store to hold master copies, e.g. a fireproof safe. Only authorized media should be accepted into the DML, strictly controlled by SACM.

The DML is a foundation for **release and deployment management**.

The exact configuration of the DML is defined during the **planning** activities. The definition includes:

■ Medium, physical location, hardware and software to be used, if kept online – some **configuration management** support tools incorporate document or software libraries, which can be regarded as a logical part of a DML

■ Naming conventions for filestore areas and physical media

■ **Environments** supported, e.g. test and **live** environments

- **Security** arrangements for submitting changes and issuing documentation and software, plus **backup** and **recovery procedures**
- The **scope** of the DML, e.g. source code, object code from controlled **builds** and associated documentation
- Archive and retention periods
- **Capacity plans** for the DML and procedures for **monitoring** growth in size
- Audit **procedures**
- Procedures to ensure that the DML is protected from erroneous or unauthorized change (e.g. entry and exit criteria for items).

7.3.1.7 Definitive spares

An area should be set aside for the secure storage of definitive hardware spares. These are spare **components** and assemblies that are maintained at the same level as the comparative **systems** within the controlled test or **live environment**. Details of these components, their locations and their respective **builds** and contents should be comprehensively recorded in the CMS. These can then be used in a controlled manner when needed for additional systems or in the recovery from **incidents**. Once their (temporary) use has ended, they are returned to the spares store or replacements are obtained.

7.3.1.8 Configuration baseline

A configuration **baseline** is the configuration of a service, product or infrastructure that has been formally reviewed and agreed on, that thereafter serves as the basis for further activities and that can be changed only through formal **change procedures**. It captures the structure, contents and details of a configuration and represents a set of **configuration items** that are related to each other.

Establishing a baseline provides the ability to:
- Mark a milestone in the **development** of a service, e.g. **service design** baseline
- Build a service component from a defined set of inputs
- Change or rebuild a specific **version** at a later date
- Assemble all relevant components in readiness for a change or **release**
- Provide the basis for a configuration **audit** and back out, e.g. after a change.

7.3.1.9 Snapshot

A **snapshot** of the current state of a configuration item or an environment, e.g. from a discovery tool. This snapshot is recorded in the CMS and remains as a fixed historical **record**. Sometimes this is referred to a footprint. A snapshot is not necessarily formally reviewed and agreed on – it is just a documentation of a state, which may contain **faults** and unauthorized CIs. One example is where a snapshot is established after an installation, perhaps using a discovery tool, and later compared to the original configuration baseline.

The snapshot:
- Enables **problem management** to analyse evidence about a situation pertaining at the time **incidents** actually occurred
- Facilitates **system restore** to support **security** scanning software.

7.3.2 Configuration identification

When **planning** configuration identification it is important to:
- Define how the classes and types of assets and **configuration items** are to be selected, grouped, classified and defined by appropriate characteristics, e.g. warranties for a **service**, to ensure that they are manageable and traceable throughout their **lifecycle**
- Define the approach to identification, uniquely naming and labelling all the assets or service **components** of interest across the service lifecycle and the relationships between them
- Define the roles and responsibilities of the owner or custodian for configuration item type at each stage of its lifecycle, e.g. the **service owner** for a **service package** or **release** at each stage of the service lifecycle.

The configuration identification **process** activities are to:
- Define and document criteria for selecting configuration items and the components that compose them
- Select the configuration items and the components that compose them based on documented criteria
- Assign unique identifiers to configuration items
- Specify the relevant **attributes** of each configuration item

Figure 7.3 – *Example configuration breakdown for an end-user computing service* [36]

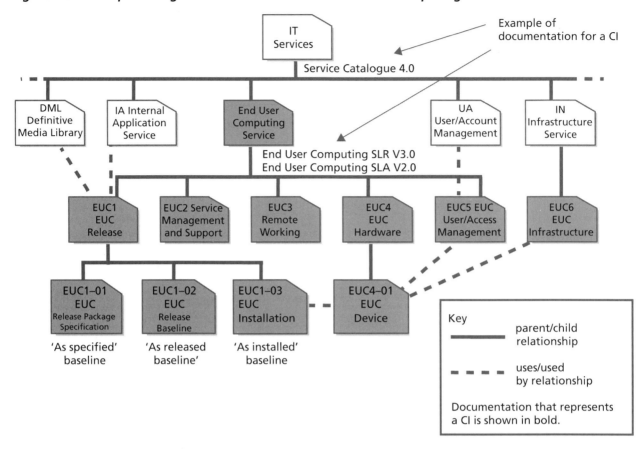

Source Service Transition was produced by OGC

■ Specify when each configuration item is placed under configuration management

■ Identify the owner responsible for each configuration item.

7.3.2.1 Configuration structures and the selection of configuration items

The configuration model should describe the relationship and position of CIs in each structure. There should be service configuration structures that identify all the components in a particular service (e.g. the retail service).

An important part of configuration management is deciding the level at which control is to be exercised, with top-level CIs broken down into components which are themselves CIs, and so on.

CIs should be selected by applying a top down approach, considering if it is sensible to break down a CI into component CIs. A CI can exist as part of any number of different CIs or CI groups at the same time. For instance, a database product may be used by many applications. Usage links to re-usable and common components of the service

should be defined – for instance, a configuration structure for a retail service will use infrastructure CIs such as servers, network and software CIs. The ability to have multiple views through different configuration structures improves accessibility, impact analysis and reporting.

Configuration management of work products and service components from the service lifecycle may be performed at several levels of granularity. The items placed under configuration management will typically include service bundles, service packages, service components, release packages and products that are delivered to the customer, designated internal work products, acquired services, products, tools, systems and other items that are used in creating and describing the configurations required to design, transition and operate the service.

Figure 7.3 gives an example in schematic representation of how a CI structure for an end-user computing service and a managed virtual system might be broken down.

Choosing the right CI level is a matter of achieving

a balance between information availability, the right level of control, and the resources and effort needed to support it. Information at a low CI level may not be valuable – for example, although a keyboard is usually exchanged independently, the organization sees it as a consumable, so does not store data about it. CI information is valuable only if it facilitates the management of change, the control of incidents and problems, or the control of assets that can be independently moved, copied or changed.

7.3.2.2 Factors that influence recording level of configuration items

The factors that affect choice of lowest CI level are not just financial. As mentioned above most organizations do not store data on keyboards because they consider them consumables, to be thrown away when not working, as one would a broken pen. However, some organizations find it worth retaining data on keyboards – for example in the United Nations, which supports many different languages within its office building, recording the specific language keyboard used is an important factor in speedy incident resolution when keyboards fail, i.e. they know which kind of replacement keyboard to send to any given user.

The organization should plan to review the CI level regularly – to confirm (or otherwise) that information down to a low level is still valuable and useful, and that the handling of changes and problems and the management of assets are not deficient because the CMDB does not go down to a sufficiently low level.

Each asset and CI needs to be uniquely identified, whether it is generated inside or outside the organization. The identification should also differentiate between successive versions and should enable the items under control to be unambiguously traceable to their specifications or equivalent, documented descriptions. Configuration descriptions and data should conform, where possible, to service, product or technology standards. Configuration data should permit forward and backward traceability to other baselined configuration states, where required.

7.4 DEMAND MANAGEMENT
7.4.1 Service packages
7.4.1.1 Core services and supporting services

Core services deliver the basic outcomes desired by the customer. They represent the value that the customer wants and for which they are willing to pay. Core services anchor the value proposition for the customer and provide the basis for their continued utilization and satisfaction. Supporting services either enable or enhance the value proposition. Enabling services are basic factors and enhancing services are excitement factors.

For example, the core service of a bank could be providing financial capital to small and medium enterprises. Value is created for the bank's customer only when the bank can provide financial capital in a timely manner (after having evaluated all the costs and risks of financing the borrower). The supporting services could include the aid offered by loan officers in assessing working capital needs and collateral, the application processing service, flexible disbursement of loan funds, and the facility of a bank account into which the borrower can electronically transfer funds. The credit-reporting service that the lending department utilizes for evaluating credit-reporting, may be a core service provided to the loan officers by internal or external service providers. It is not a supporting service to borrowers because they are not its users. Supporting services for the loan officers could include a service desk that provides technical support for the credit reporting service, email and voice mail. These services support the outcome of approving loans to credit-worthy customers in an efficient and timely manner, compliant with all policies, procedures and regulations.

In most markets, supporting services will either provide the basis for differentiation or represent the minimum requirements for operation. As excitement factors, enhancing services provide differentiation. As basic factors, enabling services only qualify the provider for an opportunity to serve customers. Enabling services are necessary for customers to utilize the core service effectively. Like basic factors, customers take their availability for granted and do not expect to be additionally charged for the value that such services provide. Examples of commonly offered enabling services are **help desk**, payment, registration, and **directory services**.

Examples of enhancing services are harder to provide because they tend to drift with time towards being subsumed into the core service or into becoming an enabling service, depending on the customer segment and **market space**. In the lending service example, the bank could provide a pre-approved banking card with which small **business** owners can make capital purchases and cover other **business** expenses. The bank can also provide a comprehensive online suite of financial management tools that allows the borrower to manage working capital and flow of funds connected to the loan account.

7.4.2 Developing differentiated offerings

The packing of core and **supporting services** is an essential aspect of market **strategy**. **Service providers** should conduct a thorough analysis of the prevailing conditions in their business **environment**, the needs of the **customer** segments or types they serve, and the alternatives that are available to those customers. The decisions are **strategic** because they hold a long-term view for maintaining value for customers even as industry practices, norms, technologies and regulations change.

Bundling of supporting services with core services has implications for the **design** and **operation** of services. Decisions have to be made whether to standardize on the core or the supporting services. One can arrive at the same level of differentiation in a service offering taking different approaches to bundling . However, the costs and **risks** involved may be different. **Service transition** processes guide such decisions. The costs and risks for supporting services may be overlooked during initial stages of **planning** and **development**. Not only that, since supporting services are often shared by several **core services**, there is often poor visibility and **control** over the demand for supporting services and their consumption.

7.4.2.1 Differentiated offerings

While service providers must focus on the effective delivery of value from core services, they should also devote enough attention to the

supporting services. Satisfaction surveys show that **user** dissatisfaction is often with supporting services even where the core service is being effectively delivered.

Some supporting services, such as **help desk** or **technical support** services typically bundled with most **service packages** can also be offered on their own. This is an important consideration in strategic planning and **reviews**. Service providers may adopt different strategies for core services and supporting services. For example, they can drive standardization and consolidation for supporting services to leverage **economies of scale** and to reduce operating costs, while developing **core service packages** specifically designed for particular customers. Or they may standardize the core service package and use supporting services to differentiate the offerings across customers or market segments. These strategic decisions can have enormous implications for the overall success of a service provider at the portfolio level. This is particularly important for service providers who need to balance the differing needs of, typically, not one but several enterprises or **business units** while trying to keep costs down across that portfolio to remain competitive.

7.4.3 Service level packages

Services packages come with one or more **service level packages** (SLP). Each SLP provides a definite level of **utility** or **warranty** from the perspective of outcomes, assets and the PBA of customers. Each SLP is capable of fulfilling one or more patterns of demand (Figure 7.3).

Figure 7.4 – Business outcomes are the ultimate basis for service level packages [37]

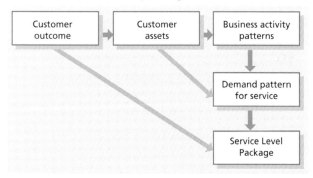

Source Service Strategy was produced by OGC

SLPs are associated with a set of **service levels**, pricing policies, and a **core service package** (CSP). CSPs are **service packages** that provide a platform of utility and warranty shared by two or more

SLPs. Combinations of CSPs and SLPs are used to serve customer segments with differentiated value. Common attributes of SLPs are subsumed into the supporting CSPs. (This is like the popular game of Tetris in which the bottom-most layer of bricks gets subsumed when all its gaps are filled with the falling bricks.) This follows the principle of modularity to reduce complexity, increase **asset** utilization across SLPs, and to reduce the overall **cost** of services. CSPs and SLPs are loosely coupled to allow for local optimization while maintaining **efficiency** over the entire supported service catalogue. Improvements made to CSPs are automatically available to all SLPs following the principle of inheritance and encapsulation. Economy of scale and economy of **scope** are realized at the CSP level and the savings are transmitted to the SLP and to customers as **policy** permits.

7.4.3.1 Service level packages are a means to provide differentiated services

In certain contexts, CSPs are **infrastructure services** offered by a specialized service unit. This allows for greater economy, learning and growth from specialization. This is similar to the arrangements between product marketing groups and manufacturing.

7.4.3.2 Advantage of core service packages

Some enterprises have highly consolidated core infrastructure units that support the operations of **business units** at a very large scale with high levels of **reliability** and **performance**. An example is a global **supply chain** and logistics company famous for its brown delivery trucks and industrialized **service**. The high levels of performance and reliability translate into similar levels of **service warranty** offered to businesses and consumers on the delivery of parcels and **documents**. The strategy is tight control over **core services** used by all business units so that complexity is under control, economy of scale is extracted, and **business** outcomes are assured. Each business unit can develop SLPs based on **applications** and processes to serve their own **market spaces**, and have them hosted on top of the core infrastructure services (Figure 7.4).

From the business unit perspective, where the SLP is hosted has implications for exposure to **quality**, cost, and risks. The company is required

Figure 7.5 – Going to market with service packages [38]

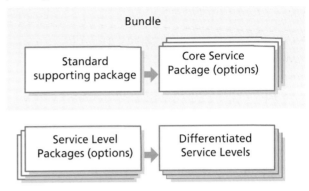

Source Service Strategy was produced by OGC

to negotiate the best possible terms for having their SLPs supported by appropriate CSPs. The principle of **separation of concerns** is applied here to increase focus on customers without compromising the economy, efficiency and stability of centralized service operations and infrastructure.

The infrastructure unit may offer their CSPs as third-party OEM services to other **service providers** who package them with their own set of SLPs. This further reduces the financial **risks** of **service assets** used to **operate** the CSP.

7.5 FINANCIAL MANAGEMENT
7.5.1 Service valuation

Service valuation quantifies, in financial terms, the funding sought by the **business** and IT for services delivered, based on the agreed value of those services. FM calculates and assigns a monetary value to a service or service **component** so that they may be disseminated across the enterprise once the **business customer** and IT identify what services are actually desired.

The **pricing** of a service is the cost-to-value translation necessary to achieve clarity and influence the demand and consumption of services. The **activity** involves identifying the **cost baseline** for services and then quantifying the perceived value added by a provider's **service assets** in order to conclude a final service value. The primary goal of service valuation is to produce a value for services that the business perceives as fair, and fulfils the needs of the provider in terms of supporting it as an ongoing concern. A secondary **objective** is the improved management of demand and consumption behaviour. It is helpful to restate what constitutes service value so that the translation to price can be more easily dissected:

'Value is created when service providers are able to deploy their capabilities and resources (i.e. service assets), and with a certain level of assurance, deliver to the customer a greater utility of their services. As established earlier, this utility is in the form of enhancing or enabling the performance of customer assets, and contributing to the realization of business outcomes.'

Within this definition, the service value elements of warranty and utility require translation of their value to an actual monetary figure. Therefore service valuation focuses primarily on two key valuation concepts:

Provisioning Value is the actual underlying cost to IT related to provisioning a service, including all fulfilment elements, both tangible and intangible. Input comes from financial systems, and consists of payment for actual resources consumed by IT in the provisioning of a service. These cost elements include items such as:

■ Hardware and software licence costs

■ Annual maintenance fees for hardware and software

■ Personnel resources used in the support or maintenance of a service

■ Utilities, data centre or other facilities charges

■ Taxes, capital or interest charges

■ Compliance costs.

The sum of these actual service costs typically represents the baseline from which the minimum value of a service is calculated since providers are seldom willing to offer a service where they are unable to recover the provisioning cost. Of course there are exceptions to this, especially related to Type I providers in situations where alternatives for provisioning of a specific service are limited or non-existent.

Service value potential is the value-added component based on the customer's perception of value from the service or expected marginal utility and warranty from using the service, in comparison with what is possible using the customer's own assets (Figure 7.5). Provisioning Value elements add up first to establish a baseline. The value-added components of the service are then monetized individually according

Figure 7.6 – Customer assets are the basis for defining value [39]

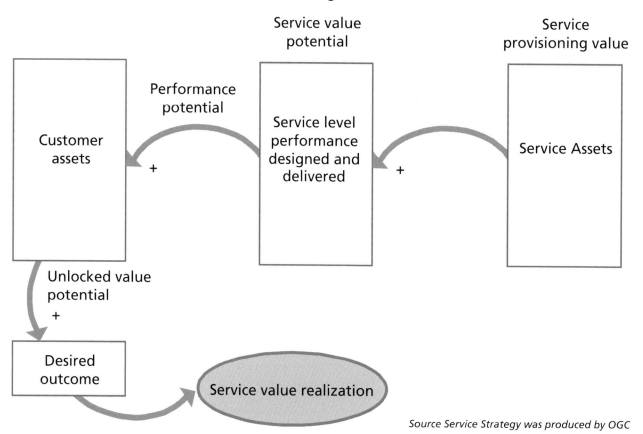

Source Service Strategy was produced by OGC

to their perceived value to estimate the true value of the service package. All of these components would then be summed along with the baseline costs to determine the ultimate value of the service. The interrelated concepts of provisioning value and perceived service value potential are illustrated in Figure 7.5.

Provisioning Value elements are typically easier to quantify due to availability of purchasing and human resources (HR) information. However, a number of techniques are available to assist with the identification of service value potential, and are addressed elsewhere in this publication and the Service Design publication. The evolution of traditional accounting methods toward a service-oriented approach that supports the decomposition and valuation of value potential components is discussed later in this section.

7.5.2 Accounting

Accounting within financial management differs from traditional accounting in that additional category and characteristics must be defined that enable the identification and tracking of service-oriented expense or capital items.

Financial management plays a translational role between corporate financial systems and service management. The result of a service-oriented accounting function is that far greater detail and understanding is achieved regarding service provisioning and consumption, and the generation of data that feeds directly into the planning process. The functions and accounting characteristics that come into play are discussed below:

■ **Service** recording – the assignment of a cost entry to the appropriate service. Depending on how services are defined, and the granularity of the definitions, there may be additional sub-service components.

■ **Cost types** – these are higher level expenses categories such as hardware, software, labour, administration, etc. These attributes assist with reporting and analysing demand and usage of services and their components in commonly used financial terms.

■ **Cost classifications** – there are also classifications within services that designate the end purpose of the cost. These include classifications such as:

■ **Capital/operational** – this classification addresses different accounting methodologies that are required by the business and regulatory agencies.

■ **Direct/indirect** – this designation determines whether a cost will be assigned directly or indirectly to a consumer or service.

  □ **Direct costs** are charged directly to a service since it is the only consumer of the expense.

  □ **Indirect** or 'shared' costs are allocated across multiple services since each service may consume a portion of the expense.

■ **Fixed/variable** – this segregation of costs is based on contractual commitments of time or price. The strategic issue around this classification is that the business should seek to optimize fixed service costs and minimize the variable in order to maximize predictability and stability.

■ **Cost units** – A cost unit is the identified unit of consumption that is accounted for a particular service or service asset.

As accounting processes and practices mature toward a service orientation, more evidence is created that substantiates the existence and performance of the IT organization. The information available by translating cost account data into service account information dramatically changes the dynamics and visibility of service management, enabling a higher level of service strategy development and execution.

7.5.3 Variable cost dynamics

Variable cost dynamics (VCD) focuses on analysing and understanding the multitude of variables that impact service cost, how sensitive those elements are to variability, and the related incremental value changes that result. Among other benefits, VCD analysis can be used to identify a marginal change in unit cost resulting from adding or subtracting one or more incremental units of a service. Such an analysis is helpful when applied toward the analysis of expected impacts from events such as acquisitions, divestitures, changes to the service portfolio or service provisioning alternatives etc.

This element of service value can be daunting since the number and type of variable elements can range dramatically depending on the type of service being analysed. The sensitivity analytics

component of variable cost dynamics is also a complex analytical tool because of the number and types of assumptions and scenarios that are often made around **variable cost** components. Below is a very brief list of possible variable service cost components that could be included in such an analysis:

- Number and type of **users**
- Number of software licences
- Cost/operating footprint of data centre
- Delivery mechanisms
- Number and type of **resources**
- The **cost** of adding one more storage device
- The cost of adding one more end-**user** licence.

The analysis of **variable cost dynamics** often follows a line of thinking similar to **market spaces**, covered elsewhere in this publication. The key value derived from this body of knowledge focuses on more precisely determining what fixed and variable cost structures are linked to a service, and how they alter based on **change** (either incremental or monumental), what the service landscape should look like as a result, how a service should be designed and provisioned, and what value should be placed on a service.

7.5.4 Methods, models, activities and techniques

This section of the chapter is intended to provide guidance in the form of sample **models**, methods, activities and techniques for key areas. The guidance provided in this section is not intended to include all possibilities or alternatives, but to provide a sampling of **best practice**.

7.5.4.1 Service valuation

During the activities of **service valuation**, regardless of the **lifecycle**, time horizon or **service** chosen, decisions will need to be made regarding various issues. This section discusses the more common points of contention that all IT centres will need to address.

Direct versus indirect costs are those that are either: 1) clearly directly attributable to a specific service, versus 2) **indirect costs** that are shared among multiple services. These costs should be approached logically to first determine which line items are sensible to maintain, given the data available and the level of effort required. For example, hardware maintenance service

components can be numerous and detailed, and it may not be of value to decompose them all for the purpose of assigning each to a line item **cost element**.

Once the depth and breadth of cost components are appropriately identified, rules or **policy** to guide how costs are to be spread among multiple services may be required. In the hardware maintenance example, rules can be created so that a percentage of the maintenance is allocated to any related services equally, or allocation rules could be based on some logical unit of consumption. Perceived equality of consumption often drives such decisions.

Labour costs are another key expenditure requiring a decision to be made. This decision is similar to that of 'direct versus indirect' above, compounded by the complexity and accuracy of time tracking **systems**. If the **capability** to account for resources allocated across services is not available, then rules and assumptions must be created for allocation of these costs. In its simplest form, organizing personnel costs across financial centres based on a service orientation is a viable method for aligning personnel costs to services. Similarly, administration costs for all IT services can be collected at a macro level within a financial centre, and rules created for allocation of this cost amongst multiple services.

Variable cost elements include expenditures that are not fixed, but which vary depending on things such as the number of **users** or the number of running instances. Decisions need to be made based on the ability to pinpoint services or service components that cause increases in variability, since this variability can be a major source of price sensitivity. Pricing variability over time can cause the need for rules to allow for predictability. Associating a cost with a highly variable service requires the ability to track specific consumption of that service over time in order to establish ranges. Predictability of that **cost** can be addressed through:

- Tiers – identifying price breaks where plateaus occur within a provider so that customers are encouraged to obtain scale efficiencies familiar to the provider.
- Maximum cost – prescribing the cost of the service based on the maximum level of

variability. This would then most likely cause overcharging, but the business may prefer 'rebates' versus additional costs.

- Average cost – this involves setting the cost of the service based on historical averaging of the variability. It would leave some amount of over- or under-charge to be addressed at the end of the planning cycle.

Translation from cost account data to service value is only possible once costs are attributed to services rather than, or in addition to, traditional cost accounts.

7.5.4.2 Translation of cost account data to service account information

This example, detailed service-oriented cost entries are captured and applied in order to establish the underlying cost **baseline** for the service (the first **component** of **service valuation**). Once this baseline has been established, monetary conversion of the value of any anticipated marginal enhancement to the **utility** and **warranty** of a customer's existing **service assets** occurs in order for the total potential value of the service to be determined.

After determining the fixed and **variable costs** for each service, steps should be taken to determine the variable cost **drivers** and range of variability for a service. This drives any additional amount that should be added to the calculation of potential service value in order to allow for absorption of consumption variability. Determining the perceived or requisite value to add to the calculation is also dependent on the operating **model** chosen since this takes into account **culture**, organization, and **strategic** direction.

Pricing the perceived value portion of a service involves resolving a grey area between historical costs, perceived value-added, and planned demand **variances**. Through this exercise, depending on the level of cost visibility present, even if actual costs are not recovered, the goal of providing cost visibility and value is demonstrated.

7.5.4.3 Chargeback: to charge or not to charge

A 'chargeback' **model** for IT can provide accountability and transparency. However, if the operating model currently provides for a more simplistic annual replenishment of funds, then **charging** is often not necessary to provide accountability or transparency. In this instance the desired visibility would instead come from the activities and outputs of **planning**, demand **modelling**, and **service valuation**. If IT is a self-funding organization, suggesting more complexity and **maturity** in financial mechanisms, then some form of charging would provide added accountability and visibility.

Visibility is brought about through identification of **service portfolios** and catalogues, valuing those **IT services**, and application of those values to demand or consumption models. Accountability refers to IT's ability to deliver expected services as agreed with the **business**, and the business's **fulfilment** of its obligations in funding those services. However, with no common ground as to what service or value the business is receiving, accountability just becomes a constant struggle to explain why perceived value varies from the funding. Therefore, charging, without taking into account the operating model, typically does not deliver desired levels of accountability and visibility.

Charging should be done to encourage behavioural changes related to steering demand for **IT services**. Charging must add value to the business and be in business terms, and it should have a degree of simplicity appropriate to the business **culture**. The most difficult and critical requirement of the model is its perceived fairness, which can be imparted if the model provides a level of predictability that the **business** typically desires, coupled with the mutual identification of services and **service** values.

Chargeback models vary based on the simplicity of the calculations and the ability for the business to understand them. Some sample chargeback models and components include:

- **Notional charging** – these chargeback alternatives address whether a journal entry will be made to the corporate financial **systems**. One option, the 'two-book' method, records costs into corporate financial systems in one fashion (for example, with IT as a **cost centre**), while a second book is kept but not recorded. This second book provides the same information but reflects what would have happened if the alternative method of recording had been used. This can be a good transitional model if chargeback practices are moving from one methodology to another.

■ Tiered subscription – involves varying levels of warranty and/or utility offered for a service or service bundle, all of which have been priced, with the appropriate chargeback models applied. Most commonly referred to as gold, silver and bronze levels of service, the weakness of tiered subscriptions is that there is no non-repudiation and it does not encourage different behaviour with regard to usage.

■ Metered usage – involves a more mature financial environment and operational capability, where demand modelling is incorporated with utility computing capabilities to provide confidence in the capture of real-time usage. This consumption information is then translated into customer charging based on various service increments that have been agreed, such as hours, days or weeks.

■ Direct Plus – this is a more simplistic model where those costs that can be attributed directly to a service are charged accordingly with some percentage of indirect costs shared amongst all.

■ Fixed or user cost – The most simplistic of chargeback models, this model takes the cost and divides by an agreed denominator such as number of users. This model contributes little to affecting customer behaviour, or identifying true service demand or consumption, but does allocate the costs to the bottom line of multiple businesses in the easiest, if somewhat inequitable, fashion if so desired.

No matter which methodology is used, or none or all, it is more important to make certain that the overriding substantiation comes from providing value to the business.

8 AFTERWORD

The Service Catalogue is not simply an IT tool. It has become central to business management as well as IT efficiency. Those implementing a Service Catalogue need to consider carefully the architecture, infrastructure and process surrounding its usage well before considering a vendor or choosing a product. The acquisition and deployment of successful Service Catalogues are not treated as internal IT tool projects, but rather projects with enterprise-wide significance.

A Service Catalogue provides access to many business services as well as IT services. The Service Catalogue is facilitating business Service Management and Service Portfolio Management—long considered the path to competitive advantage from IT. Using the Service Catalogue to provide robust automated access to IT and business services is valuable. However, understanding the patterns of business demand for services—who is consuming how much of what and at what cost—may be even more valuable. For the first time, this information, allows non-IT managers to make informed decisions regarding IT resource allocations based on demand management principles.

The central position of the Service Catalogue between business and IT makes it the logical starting point for IT budgeting, financial management, and forecasting. The Service Catalogue offers new ways to control demand, publish and track service pricing and cost, and automate service request management and fulfilment.

Of course, the contribution to the entire service lifecycle cannot be understated. A Service Catalogue provides important visualization to Service Asset and Configuration Management, as well as aiding in the assessment of business impact for Changes – all of which improves IT service quality.

Service Catalogues can help reduce costs as well. Service Catalogue looks at common ordering of PC/desktop, telecommunication, collaboration, and support services, which can produce measurable results and which assures consistent service pricing and quality. Studies show that implementing a role-driven, online, searchable Catalogue with standardized services can convert costly "information request", "status request," and "request for new service" calls into zero-cost, web-based, user self-service.

Service Catalogue also looks at ways to help reduce cycle time; implementing workflow can reduce the time it takes to fulfil services, saving numerous hours per request. Organizations can then reallocate precious staff time to more strategic initiatives.

With the introduction of ITIL v3 the Service Catalogue, and this Service Catalogue qualification, the Service Catalogue has blossomed and is now positioned as the cornerstone for IT success and increased business value.

GLOSSARY

The core publication names (*Service Strategy, Service Design, Service Operation, Service Transition, Continual Service Improvement*) included in parentheses after the name of a term indicate where a reader can find more information. Terms without an accompanying reference may be used generally in all five core publications, or may not be defined in any greater detail elsewhere. In other words, readers are only directed to other sources where they can expect to expand on their knowledge or to see a greater context.

account manager (*Service Strategy*) A role that is very similar to that of the business relationship manager, but includes more commercial aspects. Most commonly used when dealing with external customers.

accounting (*Service Strategy*) The process responsible for identifying the actual costs of delivering IT services, comparing these with budgeted costs, and managing variance from the budget.

activity A set of actions designed to achieve a particular result. Activities are usually defined as part of processes or plans, and are documented in procedures.

agreement A document that describes a formal understanding between two or more parties. An agreement is not legally binding, unless it forms part of a contract. *See also* **service level agreement**.

alert (*Service Operation*) A notification that a threshold has been reached, something has changed, or a failure has occurred. Alerts are often created and managed by system management tools and are managed by the event management process.

analytical modelling (*Continual Service Improvement*) (*Service Design*) (*Service Strategy*) A technique that uses mathematical models to predict the behaviour of IT services or other configuration items. Analytical models are commonly used in capacity management and availability management. *See also* **modelling**.

application Software that provides functions which are required by an IT service. Each application may be part of more than one IT service. An application runs on one or more servers or clients.

architecture (*Service Design*) The structure of a system or IT service, including the relationships of components to each other and to the environment they are in. Architecture also includes the standards and guidelines that guide the design and evolution of the system.

assessment Inspection and analysis to check whether a standard or set of guidelines is being followed, that records are accurate, or that efficiency and effectiveness targets are being met. *See also* **audit**.

asset (*Service Strategy*) Any resource or capability. The assets of a service provider include anything that could contribute to the delivery of a service. Assets can be one of the following types: management, organization, process, knowledge, people, information, applications, infrastructure, financial capital.

asset management (*Service Transition*) Asset management is the process responsible for tracking and reporting the value and ownership of financial assets throughout their lifecycle. Asset management is part of an overall service asset and configuration management process.

attribute (*Service Transition*) A piece of information about a configuration item. Examples are name, location, version number and cost. Attributes of CIs are recorded in the configuration management database (CMDB). *See also* **relationship**.

audit Formal inspection and verification to check whether a standard or set of guidelines is being followed, that records are accurate, or that efficiency and effectiveness targets are being met. An audit may be carried out by internal or external groups. *See also* **assessment**; **certification**.

availability (*Service Design*) Ability of an IT service or other configuration item to perform its agreed function when required. Availability is determined by reliability, maintainability, serviceability, performance and security.

Availability is usually calculated as a percentage. This calculation is often based on agreed service time and downtime. It is best practice to calculate availability of an IT service using measurements of the business output.

availability management (*Service Design*) The process responsible for defining, analysing, planning, measuring and improving all aspects of the availability of IT services. Availability management is responsible for ensuring that all IT infrastructure, processes, tools, roles etc. are appropriate for the agreed service level targets for availability.

backup (*Service Design*) (*Service Operation*) Copying data to protect against loss of integrity or availability of the original.

balanced scorecard (*Continual Service Improvement*) A management tool developed by Drs Robert Kaplan (Harvard Business School) and David Norton. A balanced scorecard enables a strategy to be broken down into key performance indicators. Performance against the KPIs is used to demonstrate how well the strategy is being achieved. A balanced scorecard has four major areas, each of which has a small number of KPIs. The same four areas are considered at different levels of detail throughout the organization.

baseline (*Continual Service Improvement*) A benchmark that is used as a reference point. For example:
- An ITSM baseline can be used as a starting point to measure the effect of a service improvement plan
- A performance baseline can be used to measure changes in performance over the lifetime of an IT service
- A configuration management baseline can be used to enable the IT infrastructure to be restored to a known configuration if a change or release fails.

benchmark
(*Continual Service Improvement*) The recorded state of something at a specific point in time. A benchmark can be created for a configuration, a process, or any other set of data. For example, a benchmark can be used in:
- Continual service improvement, to establish the current state for managing improvements

- Capacity management, to document performance characteristics during normal operations.
See also **baseline; benchmarking**.

benchmarking (*Continual Service Improvement*) Comparing a benchmark with a baseline or with best practice. The term is also used to mean creating a series of benchmarks over time, and comparing the results to measure progress or improvement.

best practice
Proven activities or processes that have been successfully used by multiple organizations. ITIL is an example of best practice.

British Standards Institution
The UK national standards body, responsible for creating and maintaining British standards. See www.bsi-global.com for more information. *See also* **International Organization for Standardization**.

budget A list of all the money an organization or business unit plans to receive, and plans to pay out, over a specified period of time. *See also* **budgeting; planning**.

budgeting The activity of predicting and controlling the spending of money. Budgeting consists of a periodic negotiation cycle to set future budgets (usually annual) and the day-to-day monitoring and adjusting of current budgets.

business (*Service Strategy*) An overall corporate entity or organization formed of a number of business units. In the context of ITSM, the term includes public sector and not-for-profit organizations, as well as companies. An IT service provider provides IT services to a customer within a business. The IT service provider may be part of the same business as its customer (internal service provider), or part of another business (external service provider).

business case (*Service Strategy*) Justification for a significant item of expenditure. The business case includes information about costs, benefits, options, issues, risks and possible problems.

business continuity management (*Service Design*) The business process responsible for managing risks that could seriously affect the business. Business continuity management safeguards the interests of key stakeholders, reputation, brand and value-creating activities. The process involves reducing risks to an acceptable level and planning for the recovery of business processes should a disruption to the business occur. Business continuity management sets the objectives, scope and requirements for IT service continuity management.

business customer (*Service Strategy*) A recipient of a product or a service from the business. For example, if the business is a car manufacturer, then the business customer is someone who buys a car.

business impact analysis (*Service Strategy*) Business impact analysis is the activity in business continuity management that identifies vital business functions and their dependencies. These dependencies may include suppliers, people, other business processes, IT services etc. Business impact analysis defines the recovery requirements for IT services. These requirements include recovery time objectives, recovery point objectives and minimum service level targets for each IT service.

business objective (*Service Strategy*) The objective of a business process, or of the business as a whole. Business objectives support the business vision, provide guidance for the IT strategy, and are often supported by IT services.

business operations (*Service Strategy*) The day-to-day execution, monitoring and management of business processes.

business perspective (*Continual Service Improvement*) An understanding of the service provider and IT services from the point of view of the business, and an understanding of the business from the point of view of the service provider.

business process A process that is owned and carried out by the business. A business process contributes to the delivery of a product or service to a business customer. For example, a retailer may have a purchasing process that helps to deliver services to its business customers. Many business processes rely on IT services.

business relationship manager (*Service Strategy*) A role responsible for maintaining the relationship with one or more customers. This role

is often combined with the service level manager role. *See also* **account manager**.

business service An IT service that directly supports a business process, as opposed to an infrastructure service, which is used internally by the IT service provider and is not usually visible to the business. The term is also used to mean a service that is delivered to business customers by business units. For example, delivery of financial services to customers of a bank, or goods to the customers of a retail store. Successful delivery of business services often depends on one or more IT services.

business service management (*Service Design*) (*Service Strategy*) An approach to the management of IT services that considers the business processes supported and the business value provided. This term also means the management of business services delivered to business customers.

business unit (*Service Strategy*) A segment of the business that has its own plans, metrics, income and costs. Each business unit owns assets and uses these to create value for customers in the form of goods and services.

call (*Service Operation*) A telephone call to the service desk from a user. A call could result in an incident or a service request being logged.

call centre (*Service Operation*) An organization or business unit that handles large numbers of incoming and outgoing telephone calls. *See also* **service desk**.

capability (*Service Strategy*) The ability of an organization, person, process, application, IT service or other configuration item to carry out an activity. Capabilities are intangible assets of an organization. *See also* **resource**.

capacity (*Service Design*) The maximum throughput that a configuration item or IT service can deliver whilst meeting agreed service level targets. For some types of CI, capacity may be the size or volume, for example a disk drive.

capacity management (*Service Design*) The process responsible for ensuring that the capacity of IT services and the IT infrastructure is able to deliver agreed service level targets in a cost-effective and timely manner. Capacity management considers all resources required to deliver the IT service, and plans for short-, medium- and long-term business requirements.

capacity planning (*Service Design*) The activity within capacity management responsible for creating a capacity plan.

capital expenditure (*Service Strategy*) The cost of purchasing something that will become a financial asset – for example, computer equipment and buildings. The value of the asset is depreciated over multiple accounting periods.

capital item (*Service Strategy*) An asset that is of interest to financial management because it is above an agreed financial value.

capitalization (*Service Strategy*) Identifying major cost as capital, even though no asset is purchased. This is done to spread the impact of the cost over multiple accounting periods. The most common example of this is software development, or purchase of a software licence.

category A named group of things that have something in common. Categories are used to group similar things together. For example, cost types are used to group similar types of cost. Incident categories are used to group similar types of incident, while CI types are used to group similar types of configuration item.

certification Issuing a certificate to confirm compliance to a standard. Certification includes a formal audit by an independent and accredited body. The term is also used to mean awarding a certificate to provide evidence that a person has achieved a qualification.

change (*Service Transition*) The addition, modification or removal of anything that could have an effect on IT services. The scope should include all IT services, configuration items, processes, documentation etc.

change case (*Service Operation*) A technique used to predict the impact of proposed changes. Change cases use specific scenarios to clarify the scope of proposed changes and to help with cost-benefit analysis. *See also* **use case.**

change management (*Service Transition*) The process responsible for controlling the lifecycle of all changes. The primary objective of change management is to enable beneficial changes to

be made, with minimum disruption to IT services.

change request *See* **request for change.**

charging (*Service Strategy*) Requiring payment for IT services. Charging for IT services is optional, and many organizations choose to treat their IT service provider as a cost centre.

classification The act of assigning a category to something. Classification is used to ensure consistent management and reporting. Configuration items, incidents, problems, changes etc. are usually classified.

client A generic term that means a customer, the business or a business customer. For example, client manager may be used as a synonym for account manager. The term is also used to mean:
■ A computer that is used directly by a user – for example, a PC, a handheld computer or a work station
■ The part of a client server application that the user directly interfaces with – for example, an e-mail client.

COBIT (*Continual Service Improvement*) Control OBjectives for Information and related Technology (COBIT) provides guidance and best practice for the management of IT processes. COBIT is published by the IT Governance Institute. *See* www.isaca.org for more information.

compliance Ensuring that a standard or set of guidelines is followed, or that proper, consistent accounting or other practices are being employed.

component A general term that is used to mean one part of something more complex. For example, a computer system may be a component of an IT service; an application may be a component of a release unit. Components that need to be managed should be configuration items.

confidentiality (*Service Design*) A security principle that requires that data should only be accessed by authorized people.

configuration (*Service Transition*) A generic term, used to describe a group of configuration items that work together to deliver an IT service, or a recognizable part of an IT service. Configuration is also used to describe the parameter settings for one or more configuration items.

Configuration Control Board (*Service Transition*) A group of people who ensure that the policies of configuration management are employed throughout the service lifecycle.

configuration management (*Service Transition*) The process responsible for maintaining information about configuration items required to deliver an IT service, including their relationships. This information is managed throughout the lifecycle of the configuration item. Configuration management is part of an overall service asset and configuration management process.

configuration management database (*Service Transition*) A database used to store configuration records throughout their lifecycle. The configuration management system maintains one or more configuration management databases, and each database stores attributes of configuration items, and relationships with other configuration items.

configuration management system (*Service Transition*) A set of tools and databases that are used to manage an IT service provider's configuration data. The configuration management system also includes information about incidents, problems, known errors, changes and releases, and may contain data about employees, suppliers, locations, business units, customers and users. The configuration management system includes tools for collecting, storing, managing, updating and presenting data about all configuration items and their relationships. The configuration management system is maintained by configuration management and is used by all IT service management processes. *See also* configuration management database; service knowledge management system.

continual service improvement (*Continual Service Improvement*) A stage in the lifecycle of an IT service and the title of one of the core ITIL publications. Continual service improvement is responsible for managing improvements to IT service management processes and IT services. The performance of the IT service provider is continually measured and improvements are made to processes, IT services and IT infrastructure in order to increase efficiency, effectiveness and cost-effectiveness. *See also* Plan–Do–Check–Act.

contract A legally binding agreement between two or more parties.

contract portfolio (*Service Strategy*) A database or structured document used to manage service contracts or agreements between an IT service provider and its customers. Each IT service delivered to a customer should have a contract or other agreement that is listed in the contract portfolio. *See also* service catalogue; service portfolio.

control A means of managing a risk, ensuring that a business objective is achieved or that a process is followed. Examples of control include policies, procedures, roles, RAID, door locks etc. A control is sometimes called a countermeasure or safeguard. Control also means to manage the utilization or behaviour of a configuration item, system or IT service.

Control Objectives for Information and related Technology *See* COBIT.

control perspective (*Service Strategy*) An approach to the management of IT services, processes, functions, assets etc. There can be several different control perspectives on the same IT service, process etc., allowing different individuals or teams to focus on what is important and relevant to their specific role. Examples of control perspective include reactive and proactive management within IT operations, or a lifecycle view for an application project team.

core service (*Service Strategy*) An IT service that delivers basic outcomes desired by one or more customers. *See also* core service package; supporting service.

core service package (*Service Strategy*) A detailed description of a core service that may be shared by two or more service level packages. *See also* service package.

cost The amount of money spent on a specific activity, IT service or business unit. Costs consist of real cost (money), notional cost (such as people's time) and depreciation.

cost centre (*Service Strategy*) A business unit or project to which costs are assigned. A cost centre does not charge for services provided. An

IT service provider can be run as a cost centre or a profit centre.

cost element (*Service Strategy*) The middle level of category to which costs are assigned in budgeting and accounting. The highest-level category is cost type. For example, a cost type of 'people' could have cost elements of payroll, staff benefits, expenses, training, overtime etc. Cost elements can be further broken down to give cost units. For example, the cost element 'expenses' could include cost units of hotels, transport, meals etc.

cost management (*Service Strategy*) A general term that is used to refer to budgeting and accounting, and is sometimes used as a synonym for financial management.

cost type (*Service Strategy*) The highest level of category to which costs are assigned in budgeting and accounting – for example, hardware, software, people, accommodation, external and transfer. *See also* cost element; cost unit.

cost unit (*Service Strategy*) The lowest level of category to which costs are assigned, cost units are usually things that can be easily counted (e.g. staff numbers, software licences) or things easily measured (e.g. CPU usage, electricity consumed). Cost units are included within cost elements. For example, a cost element of 'expenses' could include cost units of hotels, transport, meals etc. *See also* cost type.

cost-effectiveness A measure of the balance between the effectiveness and cost of a service, process or activity. A cost-effective process is one that achieves its objectives at minimum cost. *See also* return on investment; value for money.

course corrections Changes made to a plan or activity that has already started to ensure that it will meet its objectives. Course corrections are made as a result of monitoring progress.

critical success factor Something that must happen if a process, project, plan or IT service is to succeed. Key performance indicators are used to measure the achievement of each critical success factor. For example, a critical success factor of 'protect IT services when making changes' could be measured by key performance indicators such as 'percentage reduction of

unsuccessful changes', 'percentage reduction in changes causing incidents' etc.

culture A set of values that is shared by a group of people, including expectations about how people should behave, their ideas, beliefs and practices. *See also* vision.

customer Someone who buys goods or services. The customer of an IT service provider is the person or group who defines and agrees the service level targets. The term is also sometimes informally used to mean user – for example, 'This is a customer-focused organization.'

customer portfolio (*Service Strategy*) A database or structured document used to record all customers of the IT service provider. The customer portfolio is the business relationship manager's view of the customers who receive services from the IT service provider. *See also* contract portfolio; service portfolio.

Data-to-Information-to-Knowledge-to-Wisdom A way of understanding the relationships between data, information, knowledge and wisdom. DIKW shows how each of these builds on the others.

deliverable Something that must be provided to meet a commitment in a service level agreement or a contract. It is also used in a more informal way to mean a planned output of any process.

demand management Activities that understand and influence customer demand for services and the provision of capacity to meet these demands. At a strategic level, demand management can involve analysis of patterns of business activity and user profiles. At a tactical level, it can involve use of differential charging to encourage customers to use IT services at less busy times. *See also* capacity management.

dependency The direct or indirect reliance of one process or activity on another.

deployment (*Service Transition*) The activity responsible for movement of new or changed hardware, software, documentation, process etc. to the live environment. Deployment is part of the release and deployment management process.

depreciation (*Service Strategy*) A measure of

the reduction in value of an asset over its life. This is based on wearing out, consumption or other reduction in the useful economic value.

design (*Service Design*) An activity or process that identifies requirements and then defines a solution that is able to meet these requirements. *See also* service design.

detection (*Service Operation*) A stage in the incident lifecycle. Detection results in the incident becoming known to the service provider. Detection can be automatic or the result of a user logging an incident.

development (*Service Design*) The process responsible for creating or modifying an IT service or application. Also used to mean the role or group that carries out development work.

diagnosis (*Service Operation*) A stage in the incident and problem lifecycles. The purpose of diagnosis is to identify a workaround for an incident or the root cause of a problem.

direct cost (*Service Strategy*) The cost of providing an IT service which can be allocated in full to a specific customer, cost centre, project etc. For example, the cost of providing non-shared servers or software licences. *See also* indirect cost.

directory service (*Service Operation*) An application that manages information about IT infrastructure available on a network, and corresponding user access rights.

document Information in readable form. A document may be paper or electronic – for example, a policy statement, service level agreement, incident record or diagram of a computer room layout. *See also* record.

driver Something that influences strategy, objectives or requirements – for example, new legislation or the actions of competitors.

economies of scale (*Service Strategy*) The reduction in average cost that is possible from increasing the usage of an IT service or asset. *See also* economies of scope.

economies of scope (*Service Strategy*) The reduction in cost that is allocated to an IT service by using an existing asset for an additional purpose. For example, delivering a new IT service

from an existing IT infrastructure. *See also* economies of scale.

effectiveness (*Continual Service Improvement*) A measure of whether the objectives of a process, service or activity have been achieved. An effective process or activity is one that achieves its agreed objectives.

efficiency (*Continual Service Improvement*) A measure of whether the right amount of resource has been used to deliver a process, service or activity. An efficient process achieves its objectives with the minimum amount of time, money, people or other resources.

environment (*Service Transition*) A subset of the IT infrastructure that is used for a particular purpose – for example, live environment, test environment, build environment. Also used in the term 'physical environment' to mean the accommodation, air conditioning, power system etc. Environment is used as a generic term to mean the external conditions that influence or affect something.

error (*Service Operation*) A design flaw or malfunction that causes a failure of one or more IT services or other configuration items. A mistake made by a person or a faulty process that impacts a configuration item is also an error.

escalation (*Service Operation*) An activity that obtains additional resources when these are needed to meet service level targets or customer expectations. Escalation may be needed within any IT service management process, but is most commonly associated with incident management, problem management and the management of customer complaints. There are two types of escalation: functional escalation and hierarchic escalation.

e-sourcing capability model for service providers (*Service Strategy*) A framework to help IT service providers develop their IT service management capabilities from a service sourcing perspective. It was developed by Carnegie Mellon University, US.

estimation The use of experience to provide an approximate value for a metric or cost. Estimation is also used in capacity and availability management as the cheapest and least accurate modelling method.

evaluation (*Service Transition*) The process responsible for assessing a new or changed IT service to ensure that risks have been managed and to help determine whether to proceed with the change. Evaluation is also used to mean comparing an actual outcome with the intended outcome, or comparing one alternative with another.

event (*Service Operation*) A change of state that has significance for the management of an IT service or other configuration item. The term is also used to mean an alert or notification created by any IT service, configuration item or monitoring tool. Events typically require IT operations personnel to take actions, and often lead to incidents being logged.

event management (*Service Operation*) The process responsible for managing events throughout their lifecycle. Event management is one of the main activities of IT operations.

external service provider (*Service Strategy*) An IT service provider that is part of a different organization from its customer. An IT service provider may have both internal and external customers. *See also* Type III service provider.

failure (*Service Operation*) Loss of ability to operate to specification, or to deliver the required output. The term may be used when referring to IT services, processes, activities, configuration items etc. A failure often causes an incident.

failure modes and effects analysis An approach to assessing the potential impact of failures. It involves analysing what would happen after failure of each configuration item, all the way up to the effect on the business. Failure modes and effects analysis is often used in information security management and in IT service continuity planning.

fast recovery (*Service Design*) A recovery option that is also known as hot standby. Fast recovery normally uses a dedicated fixed facility with computer systems and software configured ready to run the IT services. Fast recovery typically takes up to 24 hours but may be quicker if there is no need to restore data from backups.

fault *See* error.

fault tolerance (*Service Design*) The ability of an IT service or other configuration item to continue to operate correctly after failure of a component part.

financial management (*Service Strategy*) The function and processes responsible for managing an IT service provider's budgeting, accounting and charging requirements.

fit for purpose An informal term used to describe a process, configuration item, IT service etc. that is capable of meeting its objectives or service levels. Being fit for purpose requires suitable design, implementation, control and maintenance.

fixed cost (*Service Strategy*) A cost that does not vary with IT service usage – for example, the cost of server hardware. *See also* variable cost.

follow the sun (*Service Operation*) A methodology for using service desks and support groups around the world to provide seamless 24/7 service. Calls, incidents, problems and service requests are passed between groups in different time zones.

fulfilment Performing activities to meet a need or requirement – for example, by providing a new IT service, or meeting a service request.

function A team or group of people and the tools they use to carry out one or more processes or activities – for example, the service desk. The term also has two other meanings:
- An intended purpose of a configuration item, person, team, process or IT service. For example, one function of an e-mail service may be to store and forward outgoing mails, while the function of a business process may be to despatch goods to customers.
- To perform the intended purpose correctly, as in 'The computer is functioning.'

governance Ensuring that policies and strategy are actually implemented, and that required processes are correctly followed. Governance includes defining roles and responsibilities, measuring and reporting, and taking actions to resolve any issues identified.

guideline A document describing best practice, which recommends what should be done. Compliance with a guideline is not normally enforced. *See also* standard.

help desk (*Service Operation*) A point of contact for users to log incidents. A help desk is usually more technically focused than a service desk and does not provide a single point of contact for all interaction. The term is often used as a synonym for service desk.

high availability (*Service Design*) An approach or design that minimizes or hides the effects of configuration item failure from the users of an IT service. High availability solutions are designed to achieve an agreed level of availability and make use of techniques such as fault tolerance, resilience and fast recovery to reduce the number and impact of incidents.

hot standby *See* fast recovery; immediate recovery.

immediate recovery (*Service Design*) A recovery option that is also known as hot standby. Provision is made to recover the IT service with no loss of service. Immediate recovery typically uses mirroring, load balancing and split-site technologies.

impact (*Service Operation*) (*Service Transition*) A measure of the effect of an incident, problem or change on business processes. Impact is often based on how service levels will be affected. Impact and urgency are used to assign priority.

incident (*Service Operation*) An unplanned interruption to an IT service or reduction in the quality of an IT service. Failure of a configuration item that has not yet affected service is also an incident – for example, failure of one disk from a mirror set.

incident management (*Service Operation*) The process responsible for managing the lifecycle of all incidents. The primary objective of incident management is to return the IT service to customers as quickly as possible.

indirect cost (*Service Strategy*) The cost of providing an IT service which cannot be allocated in full to a specific customer – for example, the cost of providing shared servers or software licences. Also known as overhead. *See also* direct cost.

information security management (*Service Design*) The process that ensures the confidentiality, integrity and availability of an organization's assets, information, data and IT services. Information security management usually forms part of an organizational approach to security management that has a wider scope than the IT service provider, and includes handling of paper, building access, phone calls etc. for the entire organization.

information technology The use of technology for the storage, communication or processing of information. The technology typically includes computers, telecommunications, applications and other software. The information may include business data, voice, images, video etc. Information technology is often used to support business processes through IT services.

infrastructure service An IT service that is not directly used by the business, but is required by the IT service provider so they can provide other IT services – for example, directory services, naming services or communication services.

integrity (*Service Design*) A security principle that ensures data and configuration items are modified only by authorized personnel and activities. Integrity considers all possible causes of modification, including software and hardware failure, environmental events, and human intervention.

interactive voice response (*Service Operation*) A form of automatic call distribution that accepts user input, such as key presses and spoken commands, to identify the correct destination for incoming calls.

internal rate of return (*Service Strategy*) A technique used to help make decisions about capital expenditure. It calculates a figure that allows two or more alternative investments to be compared. A larger internal rate of return indicates a better investment. *See also* net present value; return on investment.

internal service provider (*Service Strategy*) An IT service provider that is part of the same organization as its customer. An IT service provider may have both internal and external customers. *See also* Type I service provider; Type II service provider.

internal sourcing (*Service Strategy*) Using an internal service provider to manage IT services.

See also service sourcing; Type I service provider; Type II service provider.

International Organization for Standardization The International Organization for Standardization (ISO) is the world's largest developer of standards. ISO is a non-governmental organization that is a network of the national standards institutes of 156 countries. *See* www.iso.org for further information about ISO.

ISO 9000 A generic term that refers to a number of international standards and guidelines for quality management systems. *See* www.iso.org for more information. *See also* **International Organization for Standardization**.

ISO/IEC 20000 ISO specification and code of practice for IT service management. ISO/IEC 20000 is aligned with ITIL best practice.

ISO/IEC 27001 (*Continual Service Improvement*) (*Service Design*) ISO specification for information security management. The corresponding code of practice is ISO/IEC 17799. *See also* **standard**.

IT infrastructure All of the hardware, software, networks, facilities etc. that are required to develop, test, deliver, monitor, control or support IT services. The term includes all of the information technology but not the associated people, processes and documentation.

IT infrastructure library A set of best-practice guidance for IT service management. ITIL is owned by the OGC and consists of a series of publications giving guidance on the provision of quality IT services, and on the processes and facilities needed to support them. See www.itil.co.uk for more information.

IT operations (*Service Operation*) Activities carried out by IT operations control, including console management, job scheduling, backup and restore, and print and output management. IT operations is also used as a synonym for service operation.

IT operations management (*Service Operation*) The function within an IT service provider that performs the daily activities needed to manage IT services and the supporting IT infrastructure. IT operations management includes IT operations control and facilities management.

IT service A service provided to one or more customers by an IT service provider. An IT service is based on the use of information technology and supports the customer's business processes. It is made up of a combination of people, processes and technology and should be defined in a service level agreement.

IT service management The implementation and management of quality IT services that meet the needs of the business. IT service management is performed by IT service providers through an appropriate mix of people, process and information technology. *See also* **service management**.

IT service provider (*Service Strategy*) A service provider that provides IT services to internal or external customers.

job description A document that defines the roles, responsibilities, skills and knowledge required by a particular person. One job description can include multiple roles – for example, the roles of configuration manager and change manager may be carried out by one person.

Kano model (*Service Strategy*) A model developed by Noriaki Kano that is used to help understand customer preferences. The Kano model considers attributes of an IT service grouped into areas such as basic factors, excitement factors, performance factors etc.

knowledge base (*Service Transition*) A logical database containing the data used by the service knowledge management system.

knowledge management (*Service Transition*) The process responsible for gathering, analysing, storing and sharing knowledge and information within an organization. The primary purpose of knowledge management is to improve efficiency by reducing the need to rediscover knowledge. *See also* **Data-to-Information-to-Knowledge-to-Wisdom**; **service knowledge management system**.

lifecycle The various stages in the life of an IT service, configuration item, incident, problem, change etc. The lifecycle defines the categories for status and the status transitions that are permitted. For example:
- The lifecycle of an application includes

requirements, design, build, deploy, operate, optimize

■ The expanded incident lifecycle includes detect, respond, diagnose, repair, recover, restore

■ The lifecycle of a server may include: ordered, received, in test, live, disposed etc.

line of service (*Service Strategy*) A core service or supporting service that has multiple service level packages. A line of service is managed by a product manager and each service level package is designed to support a particular market segment.

maintainability (*Service Design*) A measure of how quickly and effectively an IT service or other configuration item can be restored to normal working after a failure. Maintainability is often measured and reported as MTRS. Maintainability is also used in the context of software or IT service development to mean ability to be changed or repaired easily.

managed services (*Service Strategy*) A perspective on IT services that emphasizes the fact that they are managed. The term is also used as a synonym for outsourced IT services.

management system The framework of policy, processes and functions that ensures an organization can achieve its objectives.

marginal cost (*Service Strategy*) The increase or decrease in the cost of producing one more, or one less, unit of output – for example, the cost of supporting an additional user.

market space (*Service Strategy*) All opportunities that an IT service provider could exploit to meet the business needs of customers. The market space identifies the possible IT services that an IT service provider may wish to consider delivering.

maturity (*Continual Service Improvement*) A measure of the reliability, efficiency and effectiveness of a process, function, organization etc. The most mature processes and functions are formally aligned to business objectives and strategy, and are supported by a framework for continual improvement.

mean time between failures (*Service Design*) A metric for measuring and reporting reliability. MTBF is the average time that an IT

service or other configuration item can perform its agreed function without interruption. This is measured from when the configuration item starts working, until it next fails.

mean time to repair The average time taken to repair an IT service or other configuration item after a failure. MTTR is measured from when the configuration item fails until it is repaired. MTTR does not include the time required to recover or restore. It is sometimes incorrectly used to mean mean time to restore service.

mean time to restore service The average time taken to restore an IT service or other configuration item after a failure. MTRS is measured from when the configuration item fails until it is fully restored and delivering its normal functionality. *See also* maintainability; mean time to repair.

metric (*Continual Service Improvement*) Something that is measured and reported to help manage a process, IT service or activity.

mission statement The mission statement of an organization is a short but complete description of the overall purpose and intentions of that organization. It states what is to be achieved, but not how this should be done.

model A representation of a system, process, IT service, configuration item etc. that is used to help understand or predict future behaviour.

modelling A technique that is used to predict the future behaviour of a system, process, IT service, configuration item etc. Modelling is commonly used in financial management, capacity management and availability management.

monitoring (*Service Operation*) Repeated observation of a configuration item, IT service or process to detect events and to ensure that the current status is known.

near-shore (*Service Strategy*) Provision of services from a country near the country where the customer is based. This can be the provision of an IT service, or of supporting functions such as a service desk. *See also* off-shore; on-shore.

net present value (*Service Strategy*) A technique used to help make decisions about capital expenditure. It compares cash inflows with cash outflows. Positive net present value indicates that an investment is worthwhile. *See also* **internal rate of return; return on investment.**

notional charging (*Service Strategy*) An approach to charging for IT services. Charges to customers are calculated and customers are informed of the charge, but no money is actually transferred. Notional charging is sometimes introduced to ensure that customers are aware of the costs they incur, or as a stage during the introduction of real charging.

objective The defined purpose or aim of a process, an activity or an organization as a whole. Objectives are usually expressed as measurable targets. The term is also informally used to mean a requirement. *See also* **outcome.**

Office of Government Commerce OGC owns the ITIL brand (copyright and trademark). OGC is a UK government department that supports the delivery of the government's procurement agenda through its work in collaborative procurement and in raising levels of procurement skills and capability within departments. It also provides support for complex public sector projects.

off-shore (*Service Strategy*) Provision of services from a location outside the country where the customer is based, often in a different continent. This can be the provision of an IT service, or of supporting functions such as a service desk. *See also* **near-shore; on-shore.**

on-shore (*Service Strategy*) Provision of services from a location within the country where the customer is based. *See also* **near-shore; off-shore.**

operate To perform as expected. A process or configuration item is said to operate if it is delivering the required outputs. Operate also means to perform one or more operations. For example, to operate a computer is to do the day-to-day operations needed for it to perform as expected.

operation (*Service Operation*) Day-to-day management of an IT service, system or other configuration item. Operation is also used to mean any predefined activity or transaction – for example, loading a magnetic tape, accepting money at a point of sale, or reading data from a disk drive.

operational The lowest of three levels of planning and delivery (strategic, tactical, operational). Operational activities include the day-to-day or short-term planning or delivery of a business process or IT service management process. The term is also a synonym for live.

operations management *See* IT operations management.

opportunity cost (*Service Strategy*) A cost that is used in deciding between investment choices. Opportunity cost represents the revenue that would have been generated by using the resources in a different way. For example, the opportunity cost of purchasing a new server may include not carrying out a service improvement activity that the money could have been spent on. Opportunity cost analysis is used as part of a decision-making process, but is not treated as an actual cost in any financial statement.

optimize Review, plan and request changes, in order to obtain the maximum efficiency and effectiveness from a process, configuration item, application etc.

organization A company, legal entity or other institution. Examples of organizations that are not companies include the International Standards Organization and itSMF. The term is sometimes used to refer to any entity that has people, resources and budgets –for example, a project or business unit.

outcome The result of carrying out an activity, following a process, or delivering an IT service etc. The term is used to refer to intended results, as well as to actual results. *See also* **objective.**

outsourcing (*Service Strategy*) Using an external service provider to manage IT services. *See also* **service sourcing.**

overhead *See* indirect cost.

partnership A relationship between two organizations that involves working closely together for common goals or mutual benefit. The IT service provider should have a partnership with the business and with third parties who are critical to the delivery of IT services. *See also* **value network.**

pattern of business activity (*Service Strategy*) A workload profile of one or more business activities. Patterns of business activity are used to help the IT service provider understand and plan for different levels of business activity. *See also* **user profile**.

performancemA measure of what is achieved or delivered by a system, person, team, process or IT service.

performance anatomy (*Service Strategy*) An approach to organizational culture that integrates, and actively manages, leadership and strategy, people development, technology enablement, performance management and innovation.

performance management (*Continual Service Improvement*) The process responsible for day-to-day capacity management activities. These include monitoring, threshold detection, performance analysis and tuning, and implementing changes related to performance and capacity.

pilot (*Service Transition*) A limited deployment of an IT service, a release or a process to the live environment. A pilot is used to reduce risk and to gain user feedback and acceptance. *See also* **evaluation; test**.

plan A detailed proposal that describes the activities and resources needed to achieve an objective – for example, a plan to implement a new IT service or process. ISO/IEC 20000 requires a plan for the management of each IT service management process.

Plan–Do–Check–Act (*Continual Service Improvement*) A four-stage cycle for process management, attributed to Edward Deming. Plan–Do–Check–Act is also called the Deming Cycle. Plan – design or revise processes that support the IT services; Do – implement the plan and manage the processes; Check – measure the processes and IT services, compare with objectives and produce reports; Act – plan and implement changes to improve the processes.

planning An activity responsible for creating one or more plans – for example, capacity planning.

policy Formally documented management expectations and intentions. Policies are used to direct decisions, and to ensure consistent and

appropriate development and implementation of processes, standards, roles, activities, IT infrastructure etc.

practice A way of working, or a way in which work must be done. Practices can include activities, processes, functions, standards and guidelines. *See also* **best practice**.

pricing (*Service Strategy*) Pricing is the activity for establishing how much customers will be charged.

PRINCE2 The standard UK government methodology for project management. See www.ogc.gov.uk/prince2 for more information. *See also* **Project Management Body of Knowledge**.

priority (*Service Operation*) (*Service Transition*) A category used to identify the relative importance of an incident, problem or change. Priority is based on impact and urgency, and is used to identify required times for actions to be taken. For example, the service level agreement may state that Priority 2 incidents must be resolved within 12 hours.

problem (*Service Operation*) A cause of one or more incidents. The cause is not usually known at the time a problem record is created, and the problem management process is responsible for further investigation.

problem management (*Service Operation*) The process responsible for managing the lifecycle of all problems. The primary objectives of problem management are to prevent incidents from happening, and to minimize the impact of incidents that cannot be prevented.

procedure A document containing steps that specify how to achieve an activity. Procedures are defined as part of processes.

process A structured set of activities designed to accomplish a specific objective. A process takes one or more defined inputs and turns them into defined outputs. It may include any of the roles, responsibilities, tools and management controls required to reliably deliver the outputs. A process may define policies, standards, guidelines, activities and work instructions if they are needed.

process control The activity of planning and regulating a process, with the objective of performing the process in an effective, efficient and consistent manner.

process owner A role responsible for ensuring that a process is fit for purpose. The process owner's responsibilities include sponsorship, design, change management and continual improvement of the process and its metrics. This role is often assigned to the same person who carries out the process manager role, but the two roles may be separate in larger organizations.

product manager (*Service Strategy*) A role responsible for managing one or more services throughout their entire lifecycle. Product managers are instrumental in the development of service strategy and are responsible for the content of the service portfolio.

profit centre (*Service Strategy*) A business unit that charges for services provided. A profit centre can be created with the objective of making a profit, recovering costs, or running at a loss. An IT service provider can be run as a cost centre or a profit centre.

programme A number of projects and activities that are planned and managed together to achieve an overall set of related objectives and other outcomes.

project A temporary organization, with people and other assets, that is required to achieve an objective or other outcome. Each project has a lifecycle that typically includes initiation, planning, execution, closure etc. Projects are usually managed using a formal methodology such as PRINCE2.

Project Management Body of Knowledge A project management standard maintained and published by the Project Management Institute. See www.pmi.org for more information. *See also* PRINCE2.

PRojects IN Controlled Environments *See* PRINCE2.

qualification (*Service Transition*) An activity that ensures that the IT infrastructure is appropriate and correctly configured to support an application or IT service.

quality The ability of a product, service or process to provide the intended value. For example, a hardware component can be considered to be of high quality if it performs as expected and delivers the required reliability. Process quality also requires an ability to monitor effectiveness and efficiency, and to improve them if necessary.

RACI (*Continual Service Improvement*) (*Service Design*) A model used to help define roles and responsibilities. RACI stands for responsible, accountable, consulted and informed.

record A document containing the results or other output from a process or activity. Records are evidence of the fact that an activity took place and may be paper or electronic – for example, an audit report, an incident record or the minutes of a meeting.

recovery (*Service Design*) (*Service Operation*) Returning a configuration item or an IT service to a working state. Recovery of an IT service often includes recovering data to a known consistent state. After recovery, further steps may be needed before the IT service can be made available to the users (restoration).

redundancy Use of one or more additional configuration items to provide fault tolerance. The term also has a generic meaning of obsolescence, or no longer needed.

relationship A connection or interaction between two people or things. In business relationship management, it is the interaction between the IT service provider and the business. In configuration management, it is a link between two configuration items that identifies a dependency or connection between them. For example, applications may be linked to the servers they run on, and IT services have many links to all the configuration items that contribute to that IT service.

release (*Service Transition*) A collection of hardware, software, documentation, processes or other components required to implement one or more approved changes to IT services. The contents of each release are managed, tested and deployed as a single entity.

release management (*Service Transition*) The process responsible for planning, scheduling and controlling the movement of releases to test and live environments. The primary objective of release management is to ensure that the integrity of the live environment is protected and that the correct components are released. Release management is part of the release and deployment management process.

release package (*Service Transition*) Components of an IT service that will be collectively tested and released together. Each release package may include one or more release units.

reliability (*Continual Service Improvement*) (*Service Design*) A measure of how long an IT service or other configuration item can perform its agreed function without interruption. Usually measured as MTBF or MTBSI. The term can also be used to state how likely it is that a process, function etc. will deliver its required outputs. *See also* availability.

repair (*Service Operation*) The replacement or correction of a failed configuration item.

request for change (*Service Transition*) A formal proposal for a change to be made. It includes details of the proposed change, and may be recorded on paper or electronically. The term is often misused to mean a change record, or the change itself.

requirement (*Service Design*) A formal statement of what is needed – for example, a service level requirement, a project requirement or the required deliverables for a process.

resolution (*Service Operation*) Action taken to repair the root cause of an incident or problem, or to implement a workaround. In ISO/IEC 20000, the resolution process is the process group that includes incident and problem management.

resource (*Service Strategy*) A generic term that includes IT infrastructure, people, money or anything else that might help to deliver an IT service. Resources are considered to be assets of an organization. *See also* capability; service asset.

response time A measure of the time taken to complete an operation or transaction. Used in capacity management as a measure of IT infrastructure performance, and in incident management as a measure of the time taken to answer the phone, or to start diagnosis.

responsiveness A measurement of the time taken to respond to something. This could be response time of a transaction, or the speed with which an IT service provider responds to an incident or request for change etc.

restore (*Service Operation*) Taking action to return an IT service to the users after repair and recovery from an incident. This is the primary objective of incident management.

retire (*Service Transition*) Permanent removal of an IT service, or other configuration item, from the live environment. Being retired is a stage in the lifecycle of many configuration items.

return on assets (*Service Strategy*) A measurement of the profitability of a business unit or organization. Return on assets is calculated by dividing the annual net income by the total value of assets. *See also* return on investment.

return on investment (*Continual Service Improvement*) (*Service Strategy*) A measurement of the expected benefit of an investment. In the simplest sense, it is the net profit of an investment divided by the net worth of the assets invested. *See also* net present value.

review An evaluation of a change, problem, process, project etc. Reviews are typically carried out at predefined points in the lifecycle, and especially after closure. The purpose of a review is to ensure that all deliverables have been provided, and to identify opportunities for improvement.

rights (*Service Operation*) Entitlements, or permissions, granted to a user or role – for example, the right to modify particular data, or to authorize a change.

risk A possible event that could cause harm or loss, or affect the ability to achieve objectives. A risk is measured by the probability of a threat, the vulnerability of the asset to that threat, and the impact it would have if it occurred.

risk management The process responsible for identifying, assessing and controlling risks.

role A set of responsibilities, activities and authorities granted to a person or team. A role is defined in a process. One person or team may have multiple roles – for example, the roles of configuration manager and change manager may be carried out by a single person.

scalability The ability of an IT service, process, configuration item etc. to perform its agreed function when the workload or scope changes.

scope The boundary or extent to which a process, procedure, certification, contract etc. applies. For example, the scope of change management may include all live IT services and related configuration items; the scope of an ISO/ IEC 20000 certificate may include all IT services delivered out of a named data centre.

security *See* information security management.

separation of concerns (*Service Strategy*) An approach to designing a solution or IT service that divides the problem into pieces that can be solved independently. This approach separates what is to be done from how it is to be done.

server (*Service Operation*) A computer that is connected to a network and provides software functions that are used by other computers.

service A means of delivering value to customers by facilitating outcomes customers want to achieve without the ownership of specific costs and risks. *See also* IT service.

service analytics (*Service Strategy*) A technique used in the assessment of the business impact of incidents. Service analytics models the dependencies between configuration items, and the dependencies of IT services on configuration items.

service asset Any capability or resource of a service provider. *See also* asset.

service catalogue (*Service Design*) A database or structured document with information about all live IT services, including those available for deployment. The service catalogue is the only part of the service portfolio published to customers, and is used to support the sale and delivery of IT services. The service catalogue includes information about deliverables, prices, contact points, ordering and request processes. *See also* contract portfolio.

service contract (*Service Strategy*) A contract to deliver one or more IT services. The term is also used to mean any agreement to deliver IT services, whether this is a legal contract or a service level agreement. *See also* contract portfolio.

service culture A customer-oriented culture. The major objectives of a service culture are customer satisfaction and helping customers to achieve their business objectives.

service design (*Service Design*) A stage in the lifecycle of an IT service. Service design includes a number of processes and functions and is the title of one of the core ITIL publications. *See also* design.

service desk (*Service Operation*) The single point of contact between the service provider and the users. A typical service desk manages incidents and service requests, and also handles communication with the users.

service level Measured and reported achievement against one or more service level targets. The term is sometimes used informally to mean service level target.

service level agreement (*Continual Service Improvement*) (*Service Design*) An agreement between an IT service provider and a customer. A service level agreement describes the IT service, documents service level targets, and specifies the responsibilities of the IT service provider and the customer. A single agreement may cover multiple IT services or multiple customers.

service level management (*Continual Service Improvement*) (*Service Design*) The process responsible for negotiating service level agreements, and ensuring that these are met. It is responsible for ensuring that all IT service management processes, operational level agreements and underpinning contracts are appropriate for the agreed service level targets. Service level management monitors and reports on service levels, and holds regular customer reviews.

service level package (*Service Strategy*) A defined level of utility and warranty for a particular service package. Each service level package is designed to meet the needs of a particular pattern of business activity. *See also* line of service.

service level requirement (*Continual Service Improvement*) (*Service Design*) A customer requirement for an aspect of an IT service. Service level requirements are based on business objectives and used to negotiate agreed service level targets.

service lifecycle *See* service management lifecycle.

service management Service management is a set of specialized organizational capabilities for providing value to customers in the form of services.

service management lifecycle An approach to IT service management that emphasizes the importance of coordination and control across the various functions, processes and systems necessary to manage the full lifecycle of IT services. The service management lifecycle approach considers the strategy, design, transition, operation and continuous improvement of IT services. Also known as service lifecycle.

service model (*Service Strategy*) A model that shows how service assets interact with customer assets to create value. Service models describe the structure of a service (how the configuration items fit together) and the dynamics of the service (activities, flow of resources and interactions). A service model can be used as a template or blueprint for multiple services.

service operation (*Service Operation*) A stage in the lifecycle of an IT service. Service operation includes a number of processes and functions and is the title of one of the core ITIL publications. *See also* operation.

service package (*Service Strategy*) A detailed description of an IT service that is available to be delivered to customers. A service package includes a service level package and one or more core services and supporting services.

service pipeline (*Service Strategy*) A database or structured document listing all IT services that are under consideration or development, but are not yet available to customers. The service pipeline provides a business view of possible future IT services and is part of the service portfolio that is not normally published to customers.

service portfolio (*Service Strategy*) The complete set of services that are managed by a service provider. The service portfolio is used to manage the entire lifecycle of all services, and includes three categories: service pipeline (proposed or in development), service catalogue (live or available for deployment) and retired services. *See also* contract portfolio; service portfolio management.

service portfolio management (*Service Strategy*) The process responsible for managing the service portfolio. Service portfolio management considers services in terms of the business value that they provide.

service potential (*Service Strategy*) The total possible value of the overall capabilities and resources of the IT service provider.

service provider (*Service Strategy*) An organization supplying services to one or more internal customers or external customers. Service provider is often used as an abbreviation for IT service provider. *See also* Type I service provider; Type II service provider; Type III service provider.

service provider interface (*Service Strategy*) An interface between the IT service provider and a user, customer, business process or supplier. Analysis of service provider interfaces helps to coordinate end-to-end management of IT services.

service provisioning optimization (*Service Strategy*) Analysing the finances and constraints of an IT service to decide if alternative approaches to service delivery might reduce costs or improve quality.

service reporting (*Continual Service Improvement*) The process responsible for producing and delivering reports of achievement and trends against service levels. Service reporting should agree the format, content and frequency of reports with customers.

service request (*Service Operation*) A request from a user for information or advice, for a standard change or for access to an IT service – for example, to reset a password or to provide standard IT services for a new user. Service requests are usually handled by a service desk and do not require a request for change to be submitted.

service sourcing (*Service Strategy*) The strategy and approach for deciding whether to provide a service internally or to outsource it to an external service provider. Service sourcing also means the execution of this strategy. Service sourcing includes:

- Internal sourcing – internal or shared services using Type I or Type II service providers
- Traditional sourcing – full service outsourcing using a Type III service provider
- Multi-vendor sourcing – prime, consortium or selective outsourcing using Type III service providers.

service strategy (*Service Strategy*) The title of one of the core ITIL publications. Service strategy establishes an overall strategy for IT services and for IT service management.

service transition (*Service Transition*) A stage in the lifecycle of an IT service. Service transition includes a number of processes and functions and is the title of one of the core ITIL publications. *See also* transition.

service utility (*Service Strategy*) The functionality of an IT service from the customer's perspective. The business value of an IT service is created by the combination of service utility (what the service does) and service warranty (how well it does it). *See also* utility.

service valuation (*Service Strategy*) A measurement of the total cost of delivering an IT service, and the total value to the business of that IT service. Service valuation is used to help the business and the IT service provider agree on the value of the IT service.

service warranty (*Service Strategy*) Assurance that an IT service will meet agreed requirements. This may be a formal agreement such as a service level agreement or contract, or may be a marketing message or brand image. The business value of an IT service is created by the combination of service utility (what the service does) and service warranty (how well it does it). *See also* warranty.

source *See* service sourcing.

specification A formal definition of requirements. A specification may be used to define technical or operational requirements, and may be internal or external. Many public standards consist of a code of practice and a specification. The specification defines the standard against which an organization can be audited.

stakeholder All people who have an interest in an organization, project, IT service etc. Stakeholders may be interested in the activities, targets, resources or deliverables. Stakeholders may include customers, partners, employees, shareholders, owners etc. *See also* RACI.

standard A mandatory requirement. Examples include ISO/IEC 20000 (an international standard), an internal security standard for Unix configuration, or a government standard for how financial records should be maintained. The term is also used to refer to a code of practice or specification published by a standards organization such as ISO or BSI. *See also* guideline.

standby (*Service Design*) Used to refer to resources that are not required to deliver the live IT services, but are available to support IT service continuity plans. For example, a standby data centre may be maintained to support hot standby, warm standby or cold standby arrangements.

status The name of a required field in many types of record. It shows the current stage in the lifecycle of the associated configuration item, incident, problem etc.

strategic (*Service Strategy*) The highest of three levels of planning and delivery (strategic, tactical, operational). Strategic activities include objective setting and long-term planning to achieve the overall vision.

strategy (*Service Strategy*) A strategic plan designed to achieve defined objectives.

supplier (*Service Design*) (*Service Strategy*) A third party responsible for supplying goods or services that are required to deliver IT services. Examples of suppliers include commodity hardware and software vendors, network and telecom providers, and outsourcing organizations. *See also* supply chain.

supplier management (*Service Design*) The process responsible for ensuring that all contracts with suppliers support the needs of the business, and that all suppliers meet their contractual commitments.

supply chain (*Service Strategy*) The activities in a value chain carried out by suppliers. A supply chain typically involves multiple suppliers, each adding value to the product or service. *See also* value network.

supporting service (*Service Strategy*) A service that enables or enhances a core service. For example, a directory service or a backup service. *See also* service package.

system A number of related things that work together to achieve an overall objective. For example:
■ A computer system including hardware, software and applications
■ A management system, including multiple processes that are planned and managed together – for example, a quality management system
■ A database management system or operating system that includes many software modules that are designed to perform a set of related functions.

tactical The middle of three levels of planning and delivery (strategic, tactical, operational). Tactical activities include the medium-term plans required to achieve specific objectives, typically over a period of weeks to months.

tag (*Service Strategy*) A short code used to identify a category. For example, tags EC1, EC2, EC3 etc. might be used to identify different customer outcomes when analysing and comparing strategies. The term is also used to refer to the activity of assigning tags to things.

technical management (*Service Operation*) The function responsible for providing technical skills in support of IT services and management of the IT infrastructure. Technical management defines the roles of support groups, as well as the tools, processes and procedures required.

technical support *See* technical management.

test (*Service Transition*) An activity that verifies that a configuration item, IT service, process etc. meets its specification or agreed requirements.

third party A person, group or business that is not part of the service level agreement for an IT service, but is required to ensure successful delivery of that IT service – for example, a software supplier, a hardware maintenance company or a facilities department. Requirements for third parties are typically specified in underpinning contracts or operational level agreements.

threat A threat is anything that might exploit a vulnerability. Any potential cause of an incident can be considered a threat. For example, a fire is a threat that could exploit the vulnerability of flammable floor coverings. This term is commonly used in information security management and IT service continuity management, but also applies to other areas such as problem and availability management.

threshold The value of a metric that should cause an alert to be generated or management action to be taken. For example, 'Priority 1 incident not solved within four hours', 'More than five soft disk errors in an hour', or 'More than 10 failed changes in a month'.

throughput (*Service Design*) A measure of the number of transactions or other operations performed in a fixed time – for example, 5,000 e-mails sent per hour, or 200 disk I/Os per second.

total cost of ownership (*Service Strategy*) A methodology used to help make investment decisions. It assesses the full lifecycle cost of owning a configuration item, not just the initial cost or purchase price. *See also* total cost of utilization.

total cost of utilization (*Service Strategy*) A methodology used to help make investment and service sourcing decisions. Total cost of utilization assesses the full lifecycle cost to the customer of using an IT service. *See also* total cost of ownership.

transaction A discrete function performed by an IT service – for example, transferring money from one bank account to another. A single transaction may involve numerous additions, deletions and modifications of data. Either all of these are completed successfully or none of them is carried out.

transition (*Service Transition*) A change in state, corresponding to a movement of an IT service or other configuration item from one lifecycle status to the next.

Type I service provider (*Service Strategy*) An internal service provider that is embedded within a business unit. There may be several Type I service providers within an organization.

Type II service provider (*Service Strategy*) An internal service provider that provides shared IT services to more than one business unit.

Type III service provider (*Service Strategy*) A service provider that provides IT services to external customers.

unit cost (*Service Strategy*) The cost to the IT service provider of providing a single component of an IT service. For example, the cost of a single desktop PC, or of a single transaction.

usability (*Service Design*) The ease with which an application, product or IT service can be used. Usability requirements are often included in a statement of requirements.

use case (*Service Design*) A technique used to define required functionality and objectives, and to design tests. Use cases define realistic scenarios that describe interactions between users and an IT service or other system. *See also* change case.

user A person who uses the IT service on a day-to-day basis. Users are distinct from customers, as some customers do not use the IT service directly.

user profile (*Service Strategy*) A pattern of user demand for IT services. Each user profile includes one or more patterns of business activity.

utility (*Service Strategy*) Functionality offered by a product or service to meet a particular need. Utility is often summarized as 'what it does', and may be used as a synonym for service utility.

value chain (*Service Strategy*) A sequence of processes that creates a product or service that is of value to a customer. Each step of the sequence builds on the previous steps and contributes to the overall product or service. *See also* value network.

value for money An informal measure of cost-effectiveness. Value for money is often based on a comparison with the cost of alternatives.

value network (*Service Strategy*) A complex set of relationships between two or more groups or organizations. Value is generated through exchange of knowledge, information, goods or services. *See also* partnership; value chain.

variable cost (*Service Strategy*) A cost that depends on how much the IT service is used, how many products are produced, the number and type of users, or something else that cannot be fixed in advance. *See also* variable cost dynamics.

variable cost dynamics (*Service Strategy*) A technique used to understand how overall costs are affected by the many complex variable elements that contribute to the provision of IT services.

variance The difference between a planned value and the actual measured value. Commonly used in financial management, capacity management and service level management, but could apply in any area where plans are in place.

verification (*Service Transition*) An activity that ensures that a new or changed IT service, process, plan or other deliverable is complete, accurate, reliable and matches its design specification.

version (*Service Transition*) A version is used to identify a specific baseline of a configuration item. Versions typically use a naming convention that enables the sequence or date of each baseline to be identified. For example, payroll application version 3 contains updated functionality from version 2.

vision A description of what the organization intends to become in the future. A vision is created by senior management and is used to help influence culture and strategic planning.

vulnerability A weakness that could be exploited by a threat – for example, an open firewall port, a password that is never changed, or a flammable carpet. A missing control is also considered to be a vulnerability.

warranty (*Service Strategy*) A promise or guarantee that a product or service will meet its agreed requirements. Warranty is often used as a synonym for service warranty.

workload
The resources required to deliver an identifiable part of an IT service. Workloads may be categorized by users, groups of users, or functions within the IT service. This is used to assist in analysing and managing the capacity, performance and utilization of configuration items and IT services. The term is sometimes used as a synonym for throughput.

Index